# Bring Hygge To Your Life

*How to Implement a Scandinavian Lifestyle and Make Your Home The Best Place*

STACY COLLINS

# DEDICATION

For all who seek the light.

# CONTENTS

## ACKNOWLEDGMENTS

With love and warmest feelings, I'm grateful to the Danish people for giving us Hygge. Thank you for this amazing experience, which brought fresh air, reminded me who I am, and culminated in this book.

# INTRODUCTION

The modern world is full of fancy toys and many mind-blowing tourist centers that offer exhilarating experiences. Besides, we have remarkable technological achievements and breakthroughs that our predecessors could never fathom. We have the internet with its rich resources and social media to connect us together.

Indeed, cavepeople must be jealous of us. However, are we really happier than those didn't have the benefit of our technology today? Far from it! Depression, anxiety, and other psychological disorders are ravaging the lives of many people. According to the World Health Organization, over 264 million people worldwide suffer from depression[i] The statistic is staggering. If you think that depression is a function of poverty, you're wrong. Many celebrities around the world have reported at different times that they're battling negative emotions. It's true that poverty contributes to sadness, but there are many people around the world who are living happy and fulfilled lives despite the lack of basic needs.

Please note that depression often leads to suicidal ideations, which are on the rise. There are many reasons people suffer from depression and anxiety. One of them is a lack of organization and simplicity in life. A key way of demonstrating this deficiency is the arrangement of your home. Your lack of productivity and heightened stress can be triggered because of the negative vibe of your home.

Every house has its energy. If you think it through, you'll realize that there are places you went to and you felt like staying there forever. Indeed, the people living in a place contribute to how welcoming you feel there. However, every home has its own ambiance and unique vibe. The atmosphere of a home can make you feel comfortable, without anyone uttering a word.

You can make your home that safe haven by some little tweaks here and there. When your home is cozy, it provides the perfect platform you need to think and make plans for a productive day. The energy of your home can drain out your creativity, which impairs your performance. So, it's vital that you're deliberate about creating the perfect atmosphere in your home. The idea of making your home cozy to live a happy and meaningful life is the Hygge philosophy. If you have wanted to make changes in your home that will enable you to generate positive vibes, this book is for you! This book contains tips and hacks that will guide you to create a comfortable home that supports your mental, spiritual, socioemotional, and physical health.

You can trust me to take you through this life-transforming experience. Indeed, I have these attributes, but those aren't the reasons anyone should trust a person to give them useful information. Instead, you can be confident in my ability since I've been actively practicing the Hygge philosophy for over 20 with remarkable results.

I'm very cultured with a proactive point of view for all occurrences in my life. In my early 20s into my late 30s, I traveled the world to learn many domestic hacks from different nations. I've been implementing the things I learned since then, and I'm 45 years old now, so I've acquired rich experience when it comes to making a home a home indeed.

My journeys to Denmark, in particular, have greatly inspired my commitment to helping others enjoy a cozy atmosphere in their homes. That nation is one of the best in the world when it comes to practicing the Hygge philosophy. Many people there have internalized the idea of inside calm, happiness, and the attitude of delightful meaning. Many people in the West are still missing out on these vital virtues.

Personally, it took me a while to realize that these are the most important things in life. I changed apartments at different times until I finally settled in New York. I felt something was missing in my life until I started practicing this idea. I made the necessary changes in my home, and I have a new lease on my life now. I feel it's quite selfish of me if I don't share my secrets to living a happy and meaningful life with others. It's this conviction that has given birth to this project.

So, you'll gain a detailed, mindful, practical, meticulously researched, and systematic guide regarding how to implement the Hygge philosophy. This book will help you to make the requisite changes in your home for a happier and fulfilled life. Therefore, if you have been battling stress symptoms or you don't like your home, this material is for you!

If you have a small house or apartment you want to make your little paradise, you're totally reading the right book. The book contains tips that will give you direction in your decision-making about home arrangement. This guide is also for people who are living in megacities like me on a hi-speed level. It's easy to be under immense pressure to keep up with the pace of such locations.

In such places, you have to be in charge of your life to make deliberate decisions to keep your sanity. If you aren't careful, you'll live your life at such a high speed that you'll have a disorganized home full of clutter. Meanwhile, when your home isn't comfortable, it's an additional source of stress.

This guide will also help you if you've recently moved to a new place or have plans to do that. Moving to a new place is the perfect opportunity for a new beginning. I mean, you'll be able to put your home in order from the onset. Once you achieve a solid footing, it'll require little changes and a maintenance culture in the long run.

You'll also find this book valuable if you're a homemaker or about to be one. The onus is on you to make your home a place your family loves to be. Indeed, many people wish to make their home cozy for them and welcoming to guests. However, they don't know how to go about it. I'm fully aware of this gap in knowledge, and that's why I've compiled this material together.

The amazing thing about creating a positive atmosphere in your home is that it costs almost nothing. You might have to buy some things, but you'll never have to break the bank to get them. It's more about know-how rather than having the budget to finance it. The irony of life is that people prefer to spend a lot of money on things that do not offer satisfaction. Meanwhile, many things that offer happiness and serenity are free.

You might think that you understand the value of a comfortable home. Nonetheless, you can't fully realize its essence until you experience it. For example, my friend was often grumpy and complained a lot. During one of my visits to his home, I could tell the source of most of his frustration. I found his items flying around the house. I decided to start helping him put some of his things in the right place. My action inspired him to join in, and together we gave him somewhere he could call home.

He realized that people who came to visit him were staying longer after he turned his home around. He has more friends now, and he has been calmer since then. I'm not in any way suggesting that the only source of frustration and stress is a disorganized home. Indeed, many factors can be responsible for depression and anxiety. However, there's no doubt that having a home full of clutter can be detrimental to your psychological and physical health.

More so, I'm not saying that practicing the Hygge philosophy will take away all your problems. Nothing in this world is a multipurpose solution that takes away every challenge. Not even a magic wand offers such an impossible ability. However, changing your culture of home arrangement and simplifying your life will definitely give you a new lease of life. It'll reduce your stress and anxiety levels, thereby improving your mental, spiritual, and physical health.

It'll also increase your calmness and clarity of mind, which boosts the quality of your decisions. So, it's vital that you start reading this book now. You'll be making a mistake if you drop it after reading the introduction. You need to leverage the information in this material to improve the quality of your life.

So, create time to read it as part of your daily schedule. Every chapter will get you closer to creating your ideal home. Blogs and articles can only offer you various bits of the hacks available in this guide. This book is a complete compilation of many years of experience and research in this field. Therefore, start reading now until you finish it, and thank me later.

# PART 1:
# WHAT'S HYGGE?

## 1 PHILOSOPHY AND MAIN PRINCIPLES OF HYGGE

Happiness is the greatest pursuit of humankind. We all desire to have the feeling of contentment and peace of mind, regardless of our social and economic status. Money can contribute to happiness. However, an individual doesn't need to have his or her name on the Forbes list of the richest people on earth to be happy.

There are many people who are just getting by but are happier and live a more meaningful life than famous people. In fact, many celebrities have confessed at one time or the other about suffering from depression. Many turn to drugs to fill the "void" in their lives. Practicing Hygge can simplify life for you and help you live a fuller life. This chapter will explore the meaning of this concept and other related ideas you need to understand.

## THE MEANING OF HYGGE

It's logical that we start this book by explaining the central theme – "Hygge." Hygge is a word that's popular in Norway and Denmark. It stands for a mood of coziness and comfort. It's the feeling of wellness and satisfaction. Although Hygge has more or less the same meaning in Danish and Norwegian culture, these set of practices is more rooted and central in Denmark than in Norway[ii]. Nonetheless, this phenomenon didn't enjoy the kind of emphasis it has today in the Danish culture until the late 20th century.

Hygge is rooted in a Danish word, which means to give comfort, courage, or joy. It stems from "hyggja" which means to think in Old Norse. This idea is built from an Old Norse word "hugr."[iii] This word was later shortened to what is called "hug" in the modern world. It can also mean mind, soul, or consciousness. Some experts argue that Hygge might have originated from the same root word for hug. Hug stems from "hugge," which was a famous word in the 1560s that meant "to embrace." Meanwhile, the word "hugge" has an unknown origin. However, it is often linked with an Old Norse term, "hygga." This word means "to comfort." Note that hygga comes from the term "hugr" which means "mood." Moreover, hugr is from

14

a German word hugyan, which has a resemblance to an Old English word "hycgan," which implies "to think, consider."

Hygge appeared in Danish writing for the first time in the 19th century. Since then, it has evolved into the cultural phenomenon popular in Norway and Denmark today. This idea has other derived forms, including Hyggelig in Denmark. As mentioned earlier, it's a common philosophy in both Denmark and Norway. However, the importance attached to it in the two nations isn't the same. In the former, it's just a regular word. Nonetheless, in the latter, it's a cultural identity.

Norwegians treat Hygge as just a word that has a similar status to "cozy" in English-speaking countries. However, it's a crucial phenomenon that's life-transforming in Danish traditions. In both countries, the word refers to "a pleasant and highly valued everyday experience of safety, equality, personal wholeness, and a spontaneous social flow" and "a form of everyday togetherness." The noun form of the term includes something cozy, nice, safe, and appealing. It's a psychological state where an individual feels in control and content.

According to the Collins English Dictionary , Hygge is a concept that originated in Denmark that means to create convivial and pleasant atmospheres, which promotes wellbeing. This definition summarizes the central facts about this word.

# THE RISE OF THE HYGGE MOVEMENT

According to the Collins English Dictionary[iv], Hygge was the runner-up as the word of the year in the UK in 2016. It was only behind "Brexit". This conclusion was made after a period in which several books were written that have this term as their fundamental idea. Examples of such books include Hygge: The Danish Art of Happiness by Marie Tourell Søderberg, The Little Book of Hygge by Meik Wiking, and The Book of Hygge: The Danish Art of Living Well by Louisa Thomsen Brits.

In 1957, The New Yorker reporter[v], Robert Shaplen, in "Letter From Copenhagen," reported that this way of life was "ubiquitous" in the city. He described how the sidewalks were filled with smiling people. They often lift their hats to each other. They express this gesture to demonstrate to the person that they wish they knew them enough. Many people who have visited Denmark are usually amazed by this unusual friendliness present in the Danish culture and often wish they have the same in their nation.

I'm in this category, and this is a major reason I'm contributing my quota to spread this philosophy. The good news is that there are many people like me who are also committed to doing the same. A British journalist, Helen Russell, the author of "The Year of Living Danishly," is also committed to this cause. According to her, Hygge is taking pleasure in the availability of gentle, soothing things. It can be cashmere socks or a delicious meal.

The international recognition and popularity of the concept of Hygge were in late 2017. There was a high increase in online searchers and a rise of the hashtag on Instagram that year. There's even a song called "Hygge" in the Broadway musical, Frozen. The central theme of this song is being happy, comfortable, and together. Jemima Davies-Smythe incorporates Hygge into a redesign of her half-brother Karl Kennedy's living room in the Australian soap opera, Neighbors. The popularity of this philosophy has been on the rise since, and it won't change any time soon.

Yet there's no English word for Hygge. This idea took America by storm a couple of years ago. However, it's often misrepresented by people who don't have a sound understanding of this concept. Some people think Hygge is all about candles, material coziness, and fuzzy blankets with Scandinavian designs. However, it's way more than that. In the Danish Culture, Hygge is the symbol of making meaningful connections. So, it can be in the form of digital detoxification where you abstain from your devices for a while to connect to your true self.

Practicing Hygge can also be as simple as spending more time with your loved ones to share and have memorable experiences. During a period when the weather is harsh, it's delightful to get cozy at home with a fuzzy blanket, set up the fireplace, and enjoy yummy treats with a cup of coffee. This is a kind of introverted paradise that is spreading across Europe like wildfire. It's the crux of a popular movement on social media with the hashtag "#selfcare".

## ESSENTIAL PRINCIPLES OF HYGGE

Hygge is trendy, and it's easy to get the wrong idea. Indeed, physical coziness with fuzzy socks and aromatic candles gets the message across. Nonetheless, it's more about the coziness of the soul. Its central idea is engaging in pleasurable activities, such as dynamic conversations and being a part of a moment where people share their views about life while maintaining mutual respect. Note that you don't have to be with other people to have the Hygge feeling. You can create such moments alone. However, being with others intensifies the emotion. According to Kristian Næsby, M.A., a visiting lecturer in the Scandinavian Studies Department at the University of Washington and a native of Denmark[vi], social interactions are the ideal situations for real Hygge. The expert explained that you can make any situation "hyggelig" by enjoying the moment. However, it's best experienced when you have people with whom you share ideas while being present in the moment.

In order to avoid getting the wrong view of Hygge, I'll summarize the essential principles. Here they are:

## #Hygge Isn't An Idea; It's A Way Of Life

Indeed, I've referred to Hygge as an idea, concept, or philosophy in this book. Other writers also do the same for various reasons. I use these words sometimes to help people who are not familiar with Hygge, especially Americans, to understand what I'm talking about. However, if you see Hygge as an idea, you won't be able to get the best out of it. As mentioned earlier, there's no direct translation for this word in English. So, pardon me when I use words such as idea, concept, or philosophy to replace it in this guide.

A Danish person will feel strange when you use any of these terms to describe Hygge because isn't an idea as far as they're concerned. In Denmark, Hygge is a way of life. According to Næsby, a Danish person will never see Hygge in that light. He explained that he'd never viewed Hygge as an idea or concept until 2015 when people started discussing it outside of Denmark. According to him, Hygge is part and parcel of how they were together in Denmark.

Naesby explained that Hygge began as a cultural movement in Denmark after the Second Schleswig War in 1864. The nation lost the war to Prussia and Austria. Many people were depressed during this period. So, the country decided to focus on rebuilding local communities and looking inward for meaning and happiness. The people stopped thinking about the problems they cannot fix but on having smaller communities where trust and understanding are the foundations.

## #It Isn't...

According to Næsby, there are some things that must not be present if you want to experience the true feeling of Hygge. It's a long list, but it's vital that you're familiar with these things to have thorough experience. The first thing on the list is that it must not involve discomfort. For example, if you have a conversation where people are arguing, such that you feel stressed and alienated, it isn't Hygge. Besides, it isn't Hygge when you're texting on your phone when you ought to be spending time with your loved ones. The fact that you spent that time checking out Scandinavian design accounts on Instagram doesn't change anything. Nonetheless, Hygge doesn't mean that you should be in a crowded place like a stadium concert. The fact that it's fun doesn't make it Hygge. It's not about a location, but the way you interact with people or the situation that counts. When it's Hygge, you'll lose awareness of the place. I mean, you can be in a restaurant with four people around a table having a conversation.

You can be so engrossed in the conversation that you forget that you're in a public place. That's Hygge. Moreover, it isn't about materialism as countless marketing campaigns would have you believe. It's also not about buying candles or soft clothing. Additionally, it isn't about transforming your home into something like an Ikea (ready-made furniture brand) catalog. Purchasing things like these is more of a show of your financial muscle. However, money cannot buy Hygge. According to Næsby, a person can experience Hygge with just a cabin in the woods.

# #Hygge Can Be Unwelcoming

Most things associated with Hygge, such as spending quality times with loved ones and enjoying the comfort of home, are positive. However, there's a part that some people, especially outsiders, don't like about it. The central theme of Hygge is closing yourself off from the world to focus inwardly. This inner world can include your small group of friends or your local community. This structure isn't bad. Nonetheless, people who aren't part of this inner circle can feel unwelcome.

According to Næsby, Danish people aren't accustomed to going out with strangers. You'll be able to relate to this if you're familiar with the Seattle Freeze. This term explains the famous belief that it's difficult to make friends in Seattle, Washington. In the same way, the Danes are perceived as closed-off people. In other words, it's challenging to get into their social circles as an outsider.

# #Hygge Isn't A Synonym For Happiness

Many articles on Hygge often claim that the Danes are the happiest people on earth because they practice Hygge. So, writers often say that you'll be happier when you add more Hygge to your life. It's true that you'll find more meaning and reasons to smile with Hygge.

> **Nonetheless, you'll be missing the point if you think you can use Hygge as a direct substitute for happiness.**

Hygge improves the mood of people, but it isn't all about being happy, according to Næsby. He explained the relationship between Hygge and happiness by saying that Danish people aren't happy because of Hygge. However, the community has many happy people because it created a society where people can practice and experience Hygge. In summary, the basic principles of Hygge include simplicity, connection to nature, relaxation, companionship, and comfort.

## EXCITING FACTS ABOUT DANISH PEOPLE

I'll conclude this chapter by exploring some fun facts about Denmark and the Danish people. It's a good gesture to talk about the people that gave Hygge to the world. Here are some exciting things about the nation and its people you'll find intriguing:

## #The Danes Are One Of The Happiest People In The World

I'm not making this up. Many surveys have shown that Danish people have the most positive energy in the world. Indeed, there are various ways of evaluating happiness. Nonetheless, researchers have gotten the same result. I've been to Denmark, as mentioned earlier, and I can testify to these facts. It's one of the places in the world you can find people engaging in conversations while smiling at one another. Besides, according to the UN World Happiness Report, Denmark is one of the happiest countries in the world[vii].

# #Danish People Don't Have A Word For "Please"

It sounds incredible, but the Danes don't have a word that can be translated into "please." So, the people don't say anything that demonstrates politeness when asking for a favor. You'll be getting it wrong if you think Danish people are disrespectful or lack courtesy because they don't say "please" when making a request. That assertion is far from the truth. Rather, the people have found other ways to make their requests in a polite manner without saying it. They leverage body language, rather than use words.

# #Denmark's Flag Is The Oldest In The World

The white stripes on a red background that comprise the Denmark flag are distinct and recognizable around the globe. This flag is the oldest in the world[viii].It originated in the 14thcentury. Legend has it that this flag was a constant feature in 1219 during the battle of Lyndanisse. The flag was believed to have inspired the Danes to victory against Latvia. It was eventually adopted as a national symbol some hundred years later.

# #The Highest Mountain In The Country Is Only 170.87 Meters Tall

Denmark is the perfect location for those who want to experience Hygge by biking with their friends and family. The location is fantastic because it enables you to bike uphill. Besides, it almost feels ridiculous to call the tallest mountain "tall." It's just around 170 meters above sea level. This height will lose by some distance if there is such a competition for the highest mountains in the globe. Interestingly, 75% of the Danes continue biking all through winter, and the nation has a Cycling Embassy.

## #Janteloven

Apart from Hygge, the Danes have other exciting concepts, and Janteloven is one of them. The Swedes have a similar philosophy. Just like Hygge, you can't use an English word to replace this concept directly. It's better explained and summarized than replaced. It's an idea that is integral to Danish traditions. It's the foundation of a culture that believes that everyone is accepted and equal. Janteloven originated from the philosophy that no one in the society should be allowed to feel that they're better than others.

# #The Danes Are Famous For Liberalism

Social media is the only platform some people have to express their opinions in some nations. However, it isn't like that in Denmark. The Danes are some of the most outspoken people in the world because it's an open society that encourages liberalism. Remember when Næsby said that the people created a community where Hygge is possible? This freedom of speech is part of what he's talking about. Being allowed to say your opinion is vital to having quality mental health.

# #More Than 50% Copenhagen Residents Cycle To And From Work Daily[ix]

When you realize that Copenhagen is the capital of the nation and the center of the designer goods universe, the fact looks strange. You might have expected more people to go to their workplaces by car. However, it isn't so in Denmark. This reality in this city shows that the Danes aren't materialistic. Therefore, it's ridiculous for anyone to think that Hygge is about buying expensive items in your home to make you happy.

# #The Danes Alphabet Has Three Additional Letters: Æ, Ø, and Å

You might have noticed one of these letters in the name of Næsby. These extra letters are one of the reasons some people believe that the Danish language is one the trickiest to learn languages. Besides, it has a bunch of silent letters and complex pronunciation. You won't find these letters in the English language. So, don't be surprised that Danish concepts such as Hygge and Janteloven cannot be directly translated into English.

# #Only 76 Of The Nation's 444 Islands Are Inhabited

Remember that I told you that Hygge isn't about attending a potentially fun event like a stadium concert. The Danes are the happiest people on earth not because they have many exciting places you can visit. For example, people don't live in most of their islands. So, the nation has more than enough opportunities for outsiders who want to go on an island gateway. The most popular locations include Ærø, Rømø, Bornholm, and Læsø. Visiting these places is fun, but it doesn't guarantee that you'll experience Hygge.

# 2 WHAT ARE THE HYGGE BENEFITS?

The world is running at high speed, and many people are caught up chasing the wind. Many never realize that the most important things in life are those things money cannot buy. In the bid to become the best in their careers, many sacrifice their relationships with their loved ones and their health. We all want to get to the top of our careers. However, is it really worth the sacrifice of your interpersonal relationships and health? The answer is simple - No.

In the effort to earn money, many people work many jobs while trying to keep up with their responsibilities as parents and spouses. Many people break down along the way just to die after losing their health. I've been mentioning some of the advantages of Hygge in parts in the introduction and previous chapter. In this section, I'll focus more on the benefits you stand to enjoy by adding more Hygge principles to your life.

## WHAT'S A HYGGE ATMOSPHERE?

In 1933, Aksel Sandemose wrote the ten rules of Jante Law to explain the psyche of his Scandinavian hometown[x] . The laws can be summarized below:

• Don't think you are anything special.
• Don't think you are as good as we are.
• Don't think you are smarter than we are.
• Don't convince yourself that you are better than we are.
• Don't think you know more than we do.

- Don't think you are more important than we are.
- Don't think you are good at anything.
- Don't laugh at us.
- Don't think anyone cares about you.
- Don't think you can teach us anything.

What's obvious from these laws is that the society is above the individual. These values permeate every structure of nations like Denmark, including their educational and political structure. These rules are the foundation of the Hygge atmosphere. It's a general feeling of being warm, cozy, and surrounded by good company. The Danes emphasize this atmosphere and always try to create it in their restaurant tables and cafes. The restaurant tables often have beautiful blankets while the cafes are often lit by candlelight.

During my stay in Denmark, my host family bought a new light fixture for their kitchen. When they installed it, they weren't pleased because it had a fluorescent glow that was more suitable to an industrial setting like the operating room. This experience showed me the value the Danish people have for the atmosphere the type of light they have generates. When we sit down for dinner, they often make a sarcastic joke about the light. Eventually, they'll turn it off in favor of candles.

The Hygge atmosphere has the following features:

# #Coziness And Inclusiveness

What creates an element of intense isolation for outsiders is the cozy and socially inclusive nature of the Hygge atmosphere. It generates a temporary shelter against competition, social stratification, and the market by uniting the people around traditional values that emphasize equality. So, when a new person or group of people with a different national identity comes around, he or she often feels unwelcome. Therefore, creating this atmosphere involves building a robust and inclusive relationship in your home or among your friends, where everyone feels comfortable and essential.

## #Homogeneity

One of the things you'll notice, as I did in Denmark, is the homogeneity of the nation. Although it's a modern country, most of the people there are Danes. You'll observe a sea of tall, beautiful blondes, making it obvious that it's a Scandinavian nation. The Hygge atmosphere places a premium on unity that makes those within that inner circle feel involved and valued. So, creating this atmosphere means treating your loved ones with respect and value, irrespective of your social, cultural, or economic status.

## #It Cannot Be Bought

Although there is a whole market dedicated to supplying goods associated with creating a Hygge atmosphere, you cannot buy Hygge. It's easy to find cozy blankets, special lamps, and candles. The warm glow of this naked flame is far more natural when compared to the harsh modern light bulb. A typical Danish home is usually filled with natural materials such as wood rugs, stone, and wood. These items are essential to creating this ambiance. So, you don't have to be wealthy to enjoy a Hygge atmosphere. Bringing some outdoors inside can make a lot of difference.

# ADVANTAGES OF ADDING MORE HYGGE TO YOUR LIFE

There's truly no point in practicing Hygge if it doesn't add value to your life. Below are some of the numerous benefits you'll enjoy by adding more Hygge to your daily routine:

## #Reduction In Anxiety

Stress is part and parcel of the modern world. Working parents, especially, have a lot of to-do lists they need to tick off daily. If care isn't taken, you can be overwhelmed and be mentally exhausted by your responsibilities. However, you can efficiently manage your schedule by leveraging the Hygge lifestyle.

It involves unwinding from a busy lifestyle and spending time with yourself in your own space, doing things at your own pace. This approach makes you be in a comfortable place where you feel in control of your environment, thereby feeling safer and less anxious.

## #Living In The Moment

Mindfulness is an Eastern idea that has become popular in the West in recent times. Its central idea is living in the moment to get the best out of every experience. This philosophy also encourages practicing gratitude. Just like mindfulness, living in the moment is an integral part of the Hygge lifestyle.

Practicing Hygge helps you to enjoy the moment and see reasons to be grateful daily. You'll better value your relationships even when you need to pay your bills. Simply grab a pen and think about all the things you're thankful for in your life to experience the Hygge atmosphere.

# #Improved Sleep

Sleepless nights are the reality many people have to cope with today. There are many factors responsible for this. It can be due to mental stress for some people. Many people turn to over-the-counter drugs to help them sleep better. However, you can naturally improve your sleep by being relaxed and calm. Meanwhile, embracing Hygge is one of the best ways you can give yourself the requisite inner tranquility that will easily lull you to sleep.

You can achieve this by giving yourself a "me" day. It's vital that you convince yourself that you need to take a breather. On that day, you can add a few drops of essential oil like lavender to your hot bath. Then grab your favorite book and enjoy good music later. You'll find it easier to sleep on such a day.

# #Enhanced Trust And Intimacy Between Friends And Family

Hygge is more than a lifestyle trend. It's actually a state of mind that offers you the platform to enjoy the moments you treasure. Immerse yourself in the experience as you play fetch with your dog or take your kids to the park. You can experience the exhilarating feeling of Hygge through these activities. It isn't about the activity but the state of your mind when doing it. When you simplify your life, you'll be able to create more quality time for your loved ones, which enhances intimacy and trust.

# #Improved Mood

Hygge doesn't happen by mistake. It's a deliberate effort to create intimacy with yourself or those in your inner cycle to make life more bearable or worthwhile. Practicing Hygge will make you slow down at different times of the day to enjoy little moments. It can be in the form of sharing a cake or coffee with a friend. It can also involve playing games with your family or riding a bike in the fresh air to enjoy nature's wealth.

# #Alertness

The way you start your day is crucial to your experience for the rest of the day. The morning is usually the quietest part of the day because it's the period before you start getting involved in stressful activities such as attending a class or business meeting. You can give yourself the much-needed alertness for the rest of the day by living Hygge. Start the day with a cup of coffee or tea in a cozy atmosphere to keep you upbeat all day long.

# #More Focus

According to Winston Churchill, when you look back on all your worries, you'll feel like an old man who sat on his deathbed, realizing that most of his fears that had caused him a lot of trouble never happened. Note that worry impairs your focus. Nonetheless, when you simplify your life by living Hygge, you'll reduce your worries, which will translate to more focus.

## #Excellent Time Management

A crucial part of the Hygge lifestyle is the knowledge of how to do practical things and giving every task your best effort. Living Hygge will inspire you to commit yourself to activities that are productive. It will also encourage you to seek ways of improving to give you a sense of purpose. This desire will help you to train yourself to manage your time more efficiently.

# 3 IS HYGGE FOR EVERYONE?

The schedule and responsibilities of some people make them wonder if they can live the Hygge life. Indeed, we all have different commitments. Nonetheless, we can all live the Hygge life if only we choose to do so. In this chapter, we'll explore why Hygge is for everyone and how you can go about it.

## HYGGE IS IN YOUR SOUL

We're designed to live the Hygge life, and that's why we experience negativities such as mental health conditions when we do otherwise. Living the Hygge life does not make you lazy. Rather, it enables you not to bite more than you can chew. It helps you to approach life in a simple way that allows you to get the most out of your life every day.

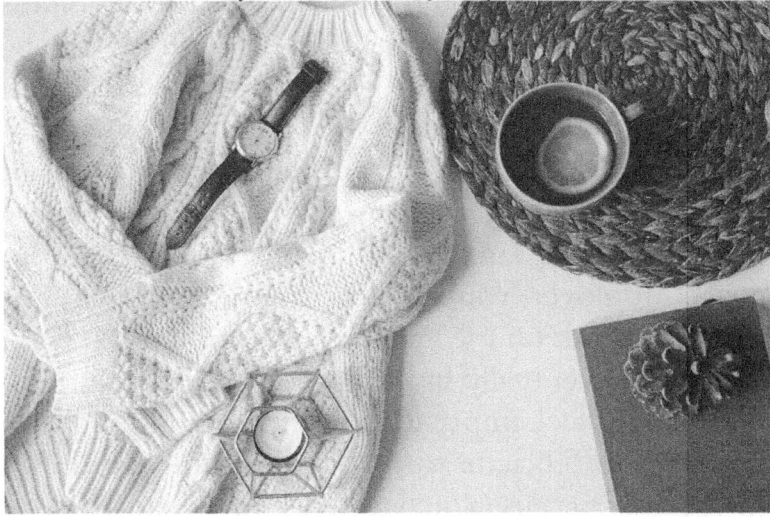

Hygge isn't for people who do not want to live a meaningful, happy, and comfortable life. Guess what?

There's no one like that! We all want to live richer and fuller lives where we can smile and have peace of mind. Many people at the top of their career live in regret because they have lost the satisfaction derived from enjoying a conversation with a friend or the warmth of a family. Meanwhile, these things are more important than fame and wealth.

Does that imply that living the Hygge life will make you a mediocre? Far from it! In fact, practicing the Hygge concept will empower you to be more effective in your career. It'll give you a clear head needed to make more quality decisions. Remember that you need to make the right choices to get the desired results. So, Hygge will boost your performance at work and in every aspect of your life. However, living the Hygge life doesn't mean that you will become the best in your field.

What Hygge offers you is contentment and happiness to enjoy your current level. There's nothing wrong with being ambitious. You should crave to be the best version of yourself. Note that ambition comes with pressure. You'll push yourself hard to achieve your goals. Nonetheless, you must not sacrifice spending time with your family and friends to achieve your goals. Moreover, you shouldn't put your mental and physical health on the line to meet your targets.

When you eventually succeed, who will celebrate with you? You'll feel empty if your friends and family do not want to felicitate with you when you succeed in your career because you haven't shown that you value them. In the same way, you'll live in regret if you cannot enjoy your success because you're sick. So, living the Hygge life gives you a work-life balance that enables you to be a success at both ends.

Nature has already wired you that way. So, don't live otherwise. As mentioned earlier, the Danes are the happiest people on earth not because they have the best economy in the world or because they have the latest gadgets. Indeed, the nation has a relatively thriving economy, and it's a typical modern state. However, the famed positive mood of the people has nothing to do with materialism. They value their loved ones and practice gratitude, which gives them a positive atmosphere for the right mood.

## WHAT PEOPLE LIVING THE HYGGE LIFE FEEL

It's sensible to understand how people living the Hygge life feel in order to evaluate whether going that way is worth it. Below are the states of mind of such people:

## #Attention To Health

People living the Hygge life prioritize their health. They understand that health is wealth. So, they don't joke with it. Note that you cannot separate your physical health from your mental health even though they aren't the same. When one is bad, it'll affect the other.

For example, when you are depressed, you won't want to participate in exercise or eat healthy foods. 'You'll only eat what is available, which can be detrimental to your well-being. In the same way, when you're physically ill, it isn't likely that you'll be happy, which leads to depression and anxiety. Living Hygge empowers you to maintain your physical, spiritual, and mental health.

# #Contentment

People living the Hygge life are not the richest in the world, but they're the most contented. Note that contentment isn't the same thing as being average. Contentment means that you'll enjoy your current status while working hard to make your situation better.

For example, if you're a new employee in a company, contentment will make you carry out your role with commitment and motivation. That doesn't mean that you don't want to become the manager someday. However, you won't feel bad about yourself because you are not yet the manager. You'll actually give the current leader your utmost support because you're content with your current role.

Contentment will help you to avoid carrying out wrong acts such as fraud or blackmail. When people are unhappy with their current situation, it often spurs them to become involved in fraudulent activities that might end up tarnishing their image or land them jail terms when caught in the act. So, living Hygge helps you to stay clear of trouble.

# #Gratitude

Gratitude is an attitude that doesn't depend on your latitude. You might appreciate the wordplay but ensure you focus on the message. What I mean is that being grateful is a state of mind that makes you have a positive mindset regardless of your current situation. It makes you always lookout for the positive during a supposedly terrible occurrence.

A person was shown a picture of a war-ravaged society, but the image was titled "peace." It sounded crazy to him because he couldn't understand what is peaceful about the picture. Then the artist showed him a corner of the image where a bird was enjoying the warmth of its loved ones inside a nest on a tree.

The artist taught him a vital lesson with the painting. He explained that peace isn't the absence of trouble. Instead, it offers inner serenity and tranquility despite being in an awful situation. The Danes learned it the hard way after losing the war. Thankfully, they're now teaching the world how to go about it. Living the Hygge life helps you to generate positive vibes by focusing on the positives in a sad or stressful situation.

## USEFUL SKILLS AND HABITS OF HYGGE

This chapter ends with how you can add more Hygge to your life. The following skills and habits will empower you to live the Hygge life:

### #Create Time For Your Loved Ones

Spending time with your friends and family improves your mood in a way that cannot be understated.

Doing it the Hygge way will make you invite them over for dinner once in a while. Discuss things you share in common, like interests in sports or politics.

You can always do this, no matter your responsibility. If you work so hard that you cannot create time for your friends and family, you'll eventually regret it. As a parent, it can affect your relationship with your kids. They can become petulant and rebellious, especially as teenagers, if you aren't there for them.

# #Reduce Time Spent In The Digital World

Digital addiction is a severe problem many people are battling around the world. Mental issues such as depression, PTSD, and fear of missing out (FOMO) are affecting many people in the modern world because they spend excessive time with their devices. Most people who claim they don't have time for hobbies or with their friends and family have time to check their social media pages. A good habit that can enable you to live Hygge is by reducing the time you spend with your digital devices. This decision will enable you to have more time for your friends and family.

# #Make The Most Of Every Moment

Living Hygge isn't possible when you're distracted. For example, when you are having a conversation with your spouse, you cannot experience Hygge when you're checking your Instagram page at the same time.

Besides, he or she can feel offended because it shows you don't value his or her availability.

In the same way, when you're eating your meal, concentrate on the food. Think about the uniqueness of taste and the creativity that produced the meal. Don't worry about your bills during that period. You'll consistently experience the Hygge feeling when you learn to stay in the moment.

# #Have Personal Times For Yourself

You'll never realize how much time you spend on irrelevant things until you take the time to evaluate your daily activities. When you "take stock," you'll realize that there are things you need to eliminate from your life that are not productive.

This action will enable you to create personal times for yourself. Just have a glass of wine or a cup of coffee and some delicious snacks during this period. Think about the success you're making and appreciate yourself as a unique individual.

Many people assume that Hygge is equivalent to cozy. Nonetheless, this isn't the case. Indeed, there are similarities. However, they aren't the same. This chapter will explore the similarities and differences between Hygge and cozy.

## SIMILARITIES BETWEEN HYGGE AND COZY

It's understandable that many people confuse Hygge with cozy because of some of the similarities they share. Here are some of the ways the two concepts go together:

### #They Both Require Intentionality

You cannot live cozy or Hygge without being deliberate. Nothing positive happens by coincidence. Even when gambling, you need to understand how the system works to increase your chances of success. So, you'll have to commit yourself to live cozy or Hygge before you can succeed in both.

Your intentionality will affect the steps you take. It's your decision that will make you create time for yourself or your friends and family. In the same way, it's your determination that will make you reduce the time you spend in the digital world or reduce clutters in your home.

### #They're Both Minimalist Concepts

Minimalism refers to simplifying your life to get the best out of it. If you're familiar with furniture design, you'll recognize that Danish brands emphasize clean, functional lines above glitter and pomp. The Danes add every object purposefully, rather than as a decorative clutter.

Hygge emphasizes simplicity, which enables you to value the most precious things in life, such as your sanity, health, peace of mind, and relationships. Meanwhile, you cannot live cozy if your home is full of unnecessary items. So, both hygge and cozy are minimalist philosophies.

# #One Can Be A Product Of The Other

Cozy can be a result of Hygge, and Hygge can lead to living cozy. In other words, your desire to enjoy your personal space to the fullest (cozy) can make you take it to the next level by living Hygge.

In the same way, your desire to simplify your life and enjoy the company of your loved one (Hygge) can make you introduce natural elements into your home and enjoy your personal time (cozy).

# #They Have Similar Goals

Whether you're living Hygge or cozy, the objective is the same. The aim of both concepts is to help you get more out of your life. The reason you want to have your personal time to treat yourself to a delicious snack and a cup of tea is that you want to remind yourself that you deserve to be loved and respected.

In the same way, the rationale that you want to light up a candle during dinner, enjoy nature, and spend quality time with your loved ones, is because you want to maintain a positive mood and live a life devoid of regrets. So, both cozy and Hygge living share the same ends.

It's vital to know the differences between living Hygge and cozy so that you'll clearly understand what you are doing. Here are some ways the two concepts differ:

# #Living Cozy Is More Individualistic Than Hygge

As earlier mentioned, you cannot have a full experience of Hygge without other people. Hygge living thrives on the trust and warmth of a close circle of friends and family. It's the national identity of the Danes that places a premium on the community.

Indeed, Hygge has elements of cozy living, such as using fluffy blankets and socks during dinner. Nonetheless, it's a practice that emphasizes the community above the individual. Personal time in Hygge living still involves spending time with your friends and family.

However, you don't need to be around people to live cozy. You can just elect to have simpler furniture in your home and reduce your clutters. Just get into your comfortable blanket, read your favorite book, and enjoy a cup of coffee. That's cozy living.

# #Cozy Living Is Simpler To Explain

Anyone can relate with living cozy because it isn't an idea that's exclusive to any nation. However, it's more challenging to explain Hygge living because it's a concept that began in the Scandinavian countries, especially Denmark. Therefore, it's strange to people who aren't from that part of the world. It often takes a person who's from Denmark or people who are acquainted with Danish traditions to have a good grasp of Hygge living.

I often see people loosely translate Hygge as cozy. However, it's a sign that such people aren't familiar with Danish culture. A person from Denmark will laugh at anyone who thinks they can explain Hygge living with a word. No word in the English vocabulary can successfully replace Hygge. So, one of the key differences between Hygge and cozy living is the simplicity of explanation of the two philosophies.

## HOW TO UNDERSTAND WHAT'S MORE SUITABLE FOR YOU

You don't have to choose between cozy living and Hygge. If you want to pick one, I've explained the differences between the two. So, you can choose whatever one you feel is more suitable for you. However, it's best to combine both of them. How can you do that? The following tips will help you:

## 1. Find A Balance Between Functionality And Happiness

You can achieve this balance by filling your home with the things you like and will use.

## 2. Reduce Over-reliance On Technology

Create a convivial environment that places a premium on well-being and comfort. Avoid digital devices that you don't need.

## 3. Don't Decorate Your Home Just For The Sake Of It

If you love decorations, it's fine, just do it. However, don't overload your home with decorative elements that can cause unnecessary clutters.

## 4. Create A Relaxing Ambiance

You can create a relaxing atmosphere in your home by employing candles and dimmers. This approach will help you and your guests enjoy staying at your house.

## 5. Slow Down When Necessary

Don't let pressure get to you and stress you out. Take things as slow as much as possible by valuing your coffee break at work and spending time with the people you love doing things that excite you.

# PART 2:
# HYGGE LIFE

This might not be the first time you are reading about Hygge life. So, you might have some level of Hyggeness in your life already. However, if this is your introduction to the concept, there's no cause for alarm. This chapter will help you to evaluate how much of Hygge you have in your life. This test will enable you to know where you are so that you can take things a notch higher from there.

## HYGGE SMART TEST

The amount of Hygge in your life is a fantastic way of measuring how happy you are. You can assess the level of Hyggeness or coziness in your life with this test below (please choose which is the most suitable for you):

***1.*** How do you usually like to spend your weekend?

a) I stay at bed all day and don't want to see anybody – **0 points**

b) I walk a lot and have outdoor activities with my friends and family – **3 points**

c) I spend all weekend to make my home clean – **1 point**

d) I visit movies, restaurants, drink wine… - **2 points**

**2.** What do you do when you have a notification on your phone when having a conversation with your loved one?

a) I pick up my phone to check it, without telling them to excuse me – **0 points**

b) I ignore it until we're done with the conversation – **3 points**

c) I check the mail then apologize to them to continue the conversation when I'm done – **1 point**

d) I ask them to excuse me to check the urgency of the alert before I continue the conversation - **2 points**

**3.** How much do you multi-task, such as checking your social media page while watching a movie?

a) So many times that I've lost count – **0 points**

b) I never do that until I'm done with what I'm doing – **3 points**

c) I rarely do that – **1 point**

d) I do that on some few occasions, especially when the movie is boring- **2 points**

**4.** How many emotionally provoking situations do you have on a typical day?

a) My life is full of them – **0 points**

b) They happen occasionally, and I can easily cope with them – **3 points**

c) I have them often, and they're hindering my mental health– **1 point**

d) They happen a number of times, and I can barely cope with them- **2 points**

**5.** How often do you find reasons to be grateful, regardless of your challenges?

a) I often get knocked down by tough situations and don't see positives – **0 points**

b) I usually take time to think about reasons to be happy even when times are hard for me – **3 points**

c) I try to find positives but often end up focusing on the negatives – **1 point**

d) I seldom find reasons to be grateful during unpleasant occurrences - **2 points**

**6.** What do you do during periods you're on break at work or less busy?

a) I'm usually with my phone checking my social media page – **0 points**

b) I enjoy a cup of coffee while having productive conversations with my colleagues – **3 points**

c) I spend the time revisiting uncompleted tasks while taking a cup of tea – **1 point**

d) I engage in conversations on various topics with my colleagues - **2 points**

**7.** How many of the items in your home do you love and use?

a) Just a few of them – **0 points**

b) All of them – **3 points**

c) Half of them – **1 point**

d) Most of them - **2 points**

**8.**   How much of natural elements do you have in your home?

a) I don't have time and space for such – **0 points**

b) I have them as much as possible – **3 points**

c) I have some, but I don't think it's necessary to have more – **1 point**

d) I have some and planning to have more - **2 points**

**9.**   How often do you have restorative baths?

a) I'm too busy to spend time taking such baths – **0 points**

b) As much as I can – **3 points**

c) Once in a while – **1 point**

d) Whenever I deem it necessary - **2 points**

**10.**   How often do you light a candle in your home to make things cozier?

a) I can't remember ever doing that at any point – **0 points**

b) I see it as an integral part of my life – **3 points**

c) I do it once in a while – **1 point**

d) I do it whenever I invite my friends and family for dinner - **2 points**

**11.**   How often do you declutter your home?

a) Never – **0 points**

b) Once in a week– **3 points**

c) Once in a month – **1 point**

d) At least twice a month - **2 points**

**12.** How frequently do you slow things down by savoring Hygge foods and beverages like coffee, baked goods, homemade soup, and mulled wine?

a) I'm usually too occupied with responsibilities to slow things down – **0 points**

b) I do that as much as I can – **3 points**

c) I slow things down whenever I'm scared I might lose my health and relationships – **1 point**

d) I often do that, but I need to be more consistent - **2 points**

**13.** What kinds of activities dominate in your life during the holiday?

a) I spend most parts learning new skills– **0 points**

b) I go hiking in nature, play board games, or ice skating with friends – **3 points**

c) I stay indoors to play games, watch movies, and sleep– **1 point**

d) I curl up with a good book alone or with my loved ones- **2 points**

**14.** How often do you leave work on time or early?

a) The nature of my work doesn't permit me to enjoy such a privilege – **0 points**

b) At least three times in a week – **3 points**

c) Once in a while – **1 point**

d) At least two times in a week - **2 points**

**15.** How many of these items do you have in your home? (A cozy throw, comfy socks, fluffy blanket, a mug, yoga pants)

a) I've never had any reasons to purchase them – **0 points**

b) Most of them – **3 points**

c) At least two of them – **1 point**

d) Some of them - **2 points**

The total marks available for this test is 45. If you **score between 39 and 45:** congratulations - you have a lot of Hygge in your life, and only have little room for improvement. However, if you have **between 30 and 38**, you have a significant level of Hygge but need to up your game. A **score between 25 and 30 demonstrates** that you have an average level of Hygge living and are in severe need of an upgrade.

Anything **less than 25** isn't worthwhile. Such an individual will be battling mental health issues or on the verge of breaking down emotionally. If you're in that category, you need to do something fast. Note that the amount of Hyggeness or coziness you have in your life says a lot about how happy you are. So, don't take it for granted if you have a low score in this test.

## WHERE TO START AND WHAT TO DO

No matter your score in this test, you can always improve. Even if you score 45 or very close to it, there are ways you can increase the level of Hyggeness or coziness in your life. Meanwhile, if you have a low score, the aim of the evaluation isn't to make you feel bad about yourself. Feeling sorry for yourself won't help matters. Rather, it'll only make things worse for you. You can start increasing the level of Hygge in your life by practicing gratitude.

The first thing you need to be grateful for is that you realize that you need to improve and are ready to make the necessary changes. Some people are unhappy with their lives but cannot identify the problems or how to fix them. So, you should see it as a positive step that you can recognize areas in your life you need to alter to have a new lease of life. It doesn't matter where you are at the moment; what matters is the commitment to get better. You have been exposed to some tips, and you'll still find more as you read on. So, start with what you know first and make the necessary changes over time. Regardless of your age, it's never too late to start living the Hygge life. Therefore, begin now!

I've been trying to explain how you can live the Hygge life from the first chapter. Indeed, living Hygge is beautiful and less stressful. It isn't a coincidence that the Scandinavian nations are the happiest people on earth. This chapter will present you with more reasons you should live the Hygge life and how you can integrate this philosophy into every aspect of your life.

## HYGGE MINDSET – WHAT DOES IT MEAN TO CHOOSE THE HYGGE?

You have the right to choose your actions, but you cannot decide the outcome of your decisions. Choosing to live Hygge has many positive results, and I have highlighted many of them. In the same way, when you opt not to apply the Hygge philosophy in your life, you'll pay the price. The truth is that I can mention the things you'll be missing. However, you can never realize how much you have missed until you start practicing the Hygge philosophy.

When you choose Hygge, you're making the following choices:

→ **Embracing Simplicity**

Life is full of complexities and complications. The pressure to be the best and meet different demands has made the life of many people complicated and difficult. Society exerts a lot of demands and expectations on us, and many end up depressed because they feel they're struggling to fulfill their potentials. However, you can choose to live your life at your pace by embracing simplicity. There's no better way to choose to live a simple life than living Hygge.

→ **Living Life On Your Own Terms**

One of the vital lessons I learned early in my life is that I always have a choice. I mean, I find many people today, when asked why they're doing something, say that they don't have a choice. This is the reason some people are in abusive relationships and mentally exhaustive jobs. There's nothing wrong with being with a person because you believe they will get better. In the same way, you can decide to stick with a job because you feel things will improve. Nonetheless, you should never say that you don't have a choice. You do! Living Hygge empowers you to live your life on your terms.

→ **Getting Your Priorities Right**

You don't have to lose your loved ones before you realize how much they mean to you. In the same way, you don't have to lose your health before you realize how integral it is to your life. Living Hygge helps you to focus on what matters the most in life – your health and relationships.

SIMPLICITY AND SLOWING DOWN

I cannot overemphasize the importance of simplicity and slowing down. These are two foundational elements of living Hygge. I picked up a lesson from a book I read some years ago that has always stayed with me. In the book, the author illustrated the importance of slowing down by telling a story of how some people busted a person's car tires because he's fond of over-speeding on their street. Indeed, the action isn't right because it's a sign of aggression.

However, the author pointed out that they did that to remind him to slow down. Then he explained that an individual should never get to a point where he loses his "tires" before he learns to reduce the pace at which he's living his life. The tires in this context can be your mental and physical health or your relationship. Many parents are living at high speed such that they never realize until it's too late.

In some cases, their teenage children are already addicted to dangerous substances or broken by misguided sexual relationships. Being too busy is also one of the reasons we have a high rate of divorce today. Some marriages are only functional but without excitements, because the couples are refusing to slow down. They have allowed other things, such as their jobs and other commitments to rob them of spending quality time with their loved ones. It often backfires in terrible ways.

So, the benefits of slowing down by taking the time to just take a breather cannot be overemphasized. It has many benefits that I won't mention, but you'll realize them as you live Hygge. It'll affect your inner tranquility, which is vital for your happiness in an increasingly crazy world. Simplicity and slowing things down doesn't mean that you won't be ambitious. Rather, it'll help you to set targets that won't require you to sacrifice your relationships and health.

## HYGGE RITUALS (MORNING, SLEEPING, DAILY)

There are many beneficial Hygge rituals that can improve the quality of your life. Here are excellent options for the morning, before you sleep, and daily.

## 5 Rituals For The Morning

The following Hygge practices will set you in the right mood for the day:

1.     Cuddle Time: Wake up early by setting your alarm so that you can have cuddle time with your children or partner.

**2.**    Get Some Calmness By Stretching: Early morning stretching is an ideal way to prepare yourself for the stress of the day.

**3.**    Pray or Meditate About The Day: Note that you don't need a religious affiliation to pray. You can start the day by declaring positive things about it.

**4.**    Beautiful Music During Shower: The soothing relief of showering with naturally scented soaps and essential oils while enjoying the melody of your favorite song is heavenly.

**5.**    Hydrate By Sipping Water Or A Cup Of Hot Tea: Put your body in the right shape hydrating with after it has gone over eight hours without fluid.

## 5 Daily Rituals

These activities will ensure that you have more reasons to smile in a day:

1. Skin Care: With a simple facial massage, you can prepare yourself for the hassle of the day. An addition of aromatherapy elements can make a lot of difference.

2. Have Your Breakfast With Your Family: You can improve your mood by taking your meal with your family before you set out.

3. Take A Walk: Taking a walk, especially in a place full of natural elements, can offer you ample opportunity to appreciate the beauty of natural design and generate positive emotions.

4. Light A Fire: Cozying up by the fireplace in your house, especially during winter, is one of the best Hygge activities you can do.

5. Light A Scented Candle: Wind down by lighting a candle that has a scent that appeals to you.

# 5 Sleeping Rituals

You'll increase your chances of sleeping like a baby when you have these sleeping rituals:

**1.** Switch Off Your Digital Devices: Science has shown that those who turn off their television and phone at least an hour before they sleep relax better than those who don't.

**2.** Candlelight Bath: A warm bath with candlelight is the perfect tonic you need to eliminate insomnia.

**3.** Use The Right Sheets And Blankets: Make your bed as comfortable as possible with a friendly layer of blankest and lots of pillows.

**4.** Appreciate The Moon: You can appreciate the beauty of nature by having a culture of saying goodnight to the moon before you sleep.

**5.** Fairy Lights: Dwell in the twinkling wonder of fairy nights before drifting off to sleep.

## COMMUNICATION IN HYGGE MEANING

Communication in Hygge means emphasizing the core components of the philosophy, such as harmony and togetherness. In friendship, it'll involve letting your friends know that you value them beyond their economic and social status. This attitude needs to shine through, especially during the days your friends do things you don't like. You'll never make them feel bad about themselves despite your disappointment. You don't need many friends because you cannot make everybody happy. However, ensure the ones you have with you don't wish they have any other person as their friends.

In a romantic or marital relationship, you'll let your partner know that he or she means the world to you. You'll use words such as "we" and "us" more predominantly than words such as "you," "I," and "me." Your words can let your spouse understand that you prize him or her above your possessions and properties. Nonetheless, your actions should also demonstrate how much your significant other means to you. You'll give your undivided attention whenever you have conversations.

In your workplace, communicating Hygge will make you eliminate competition among your employees. It's easier to do this when you're the boss. Let your workers see that they are not your subordinates but integral parts of the team. Ensure that you provide every employee with the emotional support needed to thrive in the workplace. This approach doesn't mean that you shouldn't have clear expectations from your employees. Rather, you'll set targets while specifying the roles every employee has to play to achieve organizational goals.

The way you interact with your employees is a vital way to bring Hygge into your workplace. However, you don't have to be a business owner before you can live Hygge in your office. Here are some practical ways to improve your mood in your workplace by living the Hygge life:

## → Revamp Your Work Environment

You don't have to make wholesale changes to bring Hygge to your workplace. Besides, you might not have the financial power or authority to make some alterations. However, you can make little changes that can make remarkable differences. For example, you can provide alternative lighting like lamps rather than bulbs that emit natural light. Ergonomic alternatives for stiff chairs can also reduce your job stress.

### → Avoid Multitasking

Many of us are guilty of multitasking because we want to do so much within a short period of time. It doesn't make you effective, according to experts. Besides, it affects your mental health. So, turn off unnecessary notifications at work to focus on one thing at a time. If your coworkers are less busy, you can seek their help with a task while you focus on the one at hand. This request will never be out of order, especially in a company that's built on teamwork rather than on competition.

### → Hygge Your Lunch Break

Take full advantage of your lunch break by bringing more Hygge into it. One of the ways you can do this is by sharing your meal with interested colleagues during the break. Find a serene place you can enjoy your meal without the worry of the target you need to meet. If you're the boss, you can organize group lunches to increase the bond between your employees.

## FEELING HYGGE EVERYWHERE

You can feel Hygge everywhere. It's truly all about having an open vision and seeing beauty everywhere. Hygge isn't restricted to your home or office. You can choose to live the Hygge life wherever you find yourself. Stopping by to look at the beautiful arrangement of the flowers in a garden is Hygge. Enjoying the fresh air of a clean natural environment is also a demonstration of the Hygge life.

Living Hygge is all about staying in the moment by refusing to worry about the future. The future doesn't mean the following month or year. The future also involves the next task you need to do. When you're anxious about what you need to do, it impairs your thinking, which eventually affects your performance. Meanwhile, bad performance can stifle your mood, especially if you haven't built resilience.

Life is full of unpleasant situations. However, it's also full of beautiful moments. You cannot experience these exciting moments when you aren't living the Hygge way. You cannot enjoy the taste of a delightful meal when your mind is full of the troubles in your life. Just cherish the meal and think about how to solve your problems later. The truth is that you'll always have challenges you need to resolve. If you're going to live a happy and fulfilled life, you need to take things one step at a time by immersing yourself in the current moment.

# PART 3:
# HYGGE HOME

Note that every house isn't a home. However, every home is a house. In other words, the fact that you have an expensive and luxurious apartment doesn't mean that you are happy living inside it. However, you can make your house a home indeed by bringing some Hygge ideas into it. This chapter will provide you with useful hints that will make your home a worthwhile place for you.

## DECLUTTER FREE – FIRST

One of the easiest ways you can bring Hygge into your life is to remove unnecessary items from your home. The benefits of decluttering your home include having less to clean, less debts, less stress, and many more. Below are the 10 best tips on how to declutter their home:

### Start Slowly

If you're new to the idea of decluttering, you don't need to be in a hurry. You can start by committing five minutes of your time daily to this activity. Therefore, you'll only do things that you can achieve within five minutes whenever you want to declutter your home.

### Be A Donor

You don't have to look for items you can throw into the trash can or burn. It's likely you have tons of useful stuff. So, you can help others by giving away an item per day. This approach gives you the satisfaction of adding value to other people's lives while decluttering your home. If you give one item away daily, you'll then have removed 365 excess things from your home at the end of the year.

## Fill A Trash Bag

If you're starting with five minutes a day, one of the best things you can do is employ a bag. Pick one and quickly move around your home, filling it with the things you desire to let go.

## Give Away The Clothes You Never Wear

Clothes easily become sources of clutter. So, they're excellent choices for creating more space in your home. The best way to identify the clothes you haven't worn is by hanging them in the reverse direction. When you've used one, hang it in the right order. Give away the ones you've worn before but haven't touched for a few months.

## Create A Checklist

You can make the decluttering process easier by having a visual representation of what you need to do. So, take the time to generate a checklist of all the things you will like to give away. Then donate them at different times while ticking the items on the list. You'll start from wherever you stopped anytime you wish to declutter your home again.

## Do The 12-12-12 Challenge

You can make decluttering fun by carrying it out in the form of a challenge. The 12-12-12 challenge is a fantastic way to combine creating more space with having fun. It involves identifying 12 items to discard, 12 to donate, and 12 to put back in their proper place.

## Employ The Four Box Approach

This technique is another smart and exciting way to declutter your home. It involves getting four boxes and labeling them: Give away, trash, relocate, and keep. Enter a room in your house and put each item into the right box. This method can take you a long time, but it's an effective way to know the items you should keep and the ones that should not be in your home again.

## Seek The Help Of A Friend

If you feel that decluttering your home is going to be too stressful for you, you can ask for the assistance of a friend. Let the person suggest some big items you should throw away or give away. The person will scrutinize your reason for wanting to keep any item and help you make a better decision.

# Take The Role Of A First Time Visitor

Go through your home and imagine that you are visiting the place for the first time. Like an inspector, write down the list of items that shouldn't be in your home again and the necessary changes you need to make.

# Take A Sample Picture

Take a picture of a small section of your house, like your kitchen. Then clean the place and take another picture. Compare the two images to have a view of what your home can be when you pay attention to its organization. This approach will inspire you to do more in that area.

## SPACE ORGANIZING IN HYGGE STYLE

This guide is built on Scandinavian ideas, and I've used some words rooted in that culture. It's time to be exposed to another Scandinavian word that explains space organizing in Hygge style – Lagom. This word simply means "just the right amount." In other words, it means not too much and not too small. In the context of space organizing, it implies moderation and balance in home arrangement. It's not the same as the English word "average." Rather, it refers to perfect, simple appropriateness.

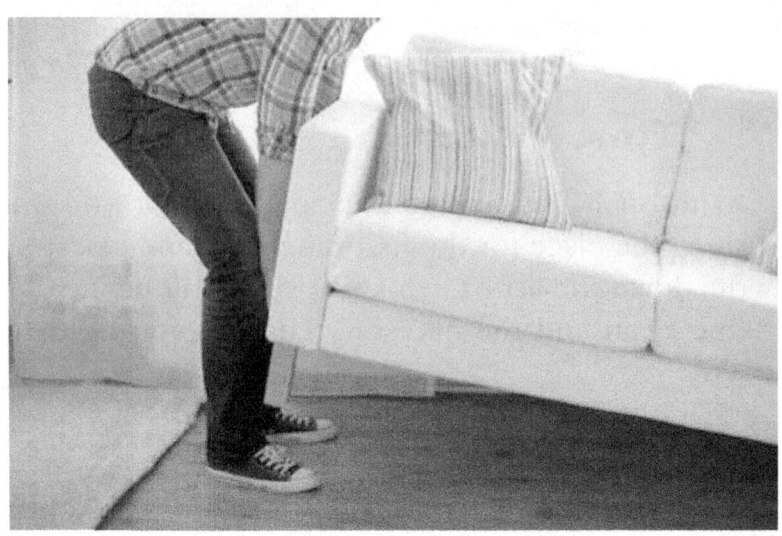

Lagom is similar to the idea that the less is more, and it's the opposite of the philosophy that the more is better. It sounds repressive for someone who isn't from the Scandinavian nations. It can make some people feel that it's an idea that is promoting mediocrity. However, for people with this national identity, it's a term that promotes consensus and equality. You can leverage this concept in space organizing by using the following tips:

## #Have A Capsule Wardrobe

A typical Scandinavian wardrobe is like a capsule. In other words, it's a minimalist, highly practical closet. It's created by clearing out undesirable or unused clothes and replacing them with a few pleasant ones. This approach will make you favor versatile clothes that you can wear in different seasons above having different clothes for various occasions.

Besides, a capsule wardrobe makes it easy to pick an outfit. Therefore, you'll be able to eliminate the stress of getting dressed. Moreover, it'll reduce the time and energy you spend on laundry. So, it's more economical and beneficial for the overall quality of your life.

# #Recycle

Lagom aims to create a sustainable environment. Therefore, practicing this idea will make you recognize the relevance of recycling. In other words, you need to know how to reuse and make used objects useful again. Besides, you have to learn to relocate old things and furniture with creativity and taste. This philosophy guarantees that you'll only purchase items that won't hurt the environment when you use them. Moreover, sustainability and energy saving will become your watchword.

# #A Premium On Simplicity And Functionality

Lagom demands that you won't have items or furniture in your home for the sake of it. This idea emphasizes harmony, versatility, and utility. So, when choosing furniture, you'll pick functional and logical ones. The Ikea brand is known for dedicating an entire line of furniture to this concept. This furniture features simple and clean lines. They're designed for practicability, resistance, and convenience. Many people find them fascinating, which explains the success of the company.

# #Avoid Perfection

The desire to be perfect has caused some people psychological problems such as obsessive-compulsive disorders. We cannot be perfect as humans, and many people need to realize that. So, Lagom isn't about making your home perfect. Rather, it's all about giving you that simple, functional home that ensures that you're comfortable and have all your basic needs. You don't need to invest in expensive furniture to have a classic home. Make it neat and tidy, and you'll be proud of it.

## HYGGE HOME ROUTINES

Hygge emphasizes healthy living. Therefore, cleaning your home is an integral part of Hygge life. Nonetheless, if making your home clean often leaves you physically and mentally exhausted, something is wrong. The following tips will help you achieve a sparkling home without feeling that you're expending a lot of energy:

→ **Create Your Own List Of Routines Objectives**

Introduce Hygge into your cleaning routine by creating a list of objectives. Accomplishing each of the targets will make you feel like a winner rather than feel like you've carried out a strenuous task. This approach brings a sense of purpose to your cleaning routine.

You'll feel like you're doing something that will benefit your life rather than doing an energy-draining activity. That mindset of doing something strenuous when cleaning is the reason many people struggle to put their home in good shape.

## → Leverage Cleaning Hacks

You cannot perform beyond the level of information at your disposal. In the internet age, there's no excuse to be ignorant about anything. There are several ways you can make cleaning less challenging. You can find cleaning hacks for your kitchen, bathroom, bedroom, or living room.

The internet is also full of tips for cleaning specific appliances like your refrigerator or oven. In the same way, there are several tips for cleaning your toilet or tubs to make the task less stressful. For example, you can remove stains from your carpet with vodka. You can also use essential oils to get a sparkling toilet.

## → Break The Routine Into Smaller Tasks

You shouldn't let your home get dirty in such a way that it becomes too cumbersome for you. However, if you find yourself in this unpleasant situation, you can still make the best of it. How? Don't try to do the cleaning all at once. That approach will make it too stressful, and there's no Hygge in that.

Instead, break the tasks into smaller categories. For example, you can focus on only your toilet in a day. Then proceed to your bedroom at another time. Do this with your routine list objective, and you'll experience Hygge while doing the activity.

## → Play Music

Music is a natural stress reliever. If you haven't been playing music while cleaning your home, you're missing a lot. Fill the air with your favorite tune while cleaning, and you can easily tell the difference. You'll feel relaxed such that you'll look forward to the next time you need to clean. This method helps you to transform cleaning from a chore to something fun.

## HOW TO BUILD HYGGE ATMOSPHERE

Home décor doesn't have to be expensive. Hygge life is about creating a safe and comfortable space for your friends and family. You can build a Hygge atmosphere in your home by taking advantage of the following hints:

## #Choose A Neutral Color Theme

If you want to create a Hygge atmosphere, you must place a premium on harmony. So, you should avoid a color scheme that's too overwhelming for your home décor. It should be essential to you that everything you add to your home helps to generate an ambiance of peace and unity.

Therefore, it's advisable that you stick to a neutral color palette to create a relaxing space. Choose pastel colors like browns, light grays, and creams to generate a comfortable area for the enjoyment of yourself and your guests.

# #Generate A Cozy Atmosphere

There's no better way to do this than by employing fluffy pillows and soft comforters in any of your favorite colors. This method will ensure that you can snuggle up on the couch with pillows and layers of blankets for a warm place to unwind. You can also consider making cozy nooks such as a love seat or window bench. These places are fantastic for relaxing with a cup of hot coffee or tea and a good book.

## #Decorate With Candles

Candles are parts and parcel of Danish tradition. Even outside of the Danish culture, many people light up candles to celebrate special occasions like their birthdays. However, you don't have to wait until a celebration to bring the cozy feeling of happy moments into your life.

The Hygge life is about generating positive vibes with every opportunity. The soft, warm glow of candles, especially several ones, cannot be replicated by artificial lights. This uniqueness makes them ideal for socializing and relaxing with friends.

# #Turn It Up With Twinkly Lights

Twinkly lights and Hygge décor are a perfect match. They are festive and cheery. However, they're far more than great additions during a celebration. Their radiance makes them suitable wherever you put them. They're a perfect fit for your living room, bedroom, or even outside patio. They're similar to candles in

Hygge décor because they offer a softer light. Besides, they provide a pleasant touch to your home design without being excessive or overwhelming.

## #Bring In Some Outdoors

Adding natural elements is one of the best ways you can create a Hygge atmosphere in your home. A minimalist design comes alive when you introduce texture. You can achieve this by incorporating warm, natural materials like wool and wood to your décor. You can also consider a variety of flowers for a brilliant pop of color here and there.

# THE SEASONAL DECORATION WHICH MAKES A HOME COZY

As mentioned earlier, living Hygge isn't being in a positive mood only during seasonal events. Nonetheless, you can take advantage of the festivals, especially in the fourth quarter of the year, to celebrate with your friends and family. You can bring some Hygge into your home during these periods by employing the following tips:

## #More Candles

The Danes burn a lot of candles because of their various benefits against artificial lights. This distinct light soothes the nerves, prevents eye fatigue, and increases concentration. So, the festivals are the best period to bring in more of this friendliness into your home. You can make things better by going for many scattered sources of light, rather than a single overhead one.

Say yes to all sorts of candles during seasonal celebrations to build a Hygge atmosphere. Put them in different places in your home, including your bedroom, kitchen, and bathroom. Use candle holders to avoid unprecedented fire accidents.

# #Myshörna

Are you ready for a new Scandinavian word? Myshörna! The holidays are the best periods to spend time with your loved ones. You may visit them or invite them over to your home. This culture is Hygge life. However, you should also make your home cozy for you during the periods you want to stay indoors. Myshörna simply means "a cozy corner." Note that there's no Hygge without a comfy place where you can relax to enjoy your favorite activities. So, it's vital that you arrange at least a secluded spot in your home full of everything synonymous with coziness. It can be a place to read a book or play a musical instrument.

# #Employ A Welcoming Effect

Hygge living isn't all about making the inside of your home relaxing and comfortable. You can make your guests feel welcome long before they step inside by utilizing friendly decorations, especially during the holiday seasons. It doesn't have to be excessive. A simple sign or a welcome mat with an inviting inscription or sent invitation postcard will do the magic. You won't need to spend a lot of money to get these items, but they make tremendous differences.

# #Add Excellent And Appealing Paintings

Beautiful paintings are a source of attraction in a home. It's common to see guests paying attention to them, especially when they visit the place for the first time. For a Hygge touch, pick paintings of natural objects such as pumpkins. An installation of colorful leaves or glittering acorns can also add the special effect you need during seasonal festivals.

## HYGGE MEAL

There are a plethora of fantastic options if you want Danish delicacies. However, this section isn't about the food but the setting of the table. You don't need to eat Scandinavian foods to live Hygge. Hygge living is an attitude, rather than about items. So, it's the way you eat that makes it Hygge or not rather than the food or drink.

The tips below will help you create a table setting for meals that support Hygge living:

## → Cute Napkins

Bring the Hygge atmosphere to your meal by employing nice napkins. You can buy one for just $1. Such napkins bring a relaxing effect to your table that makes the meal feel special, especially when you're with your loved ones.

## → Piece Of Twig Or Leaf From Nature

Adding a piece of twig or leaf is another way of beautifying the table while getting the Hygge feeling.

## → Danish Table Manners

The Danes' dining etiquette for utensils demands that you place the fork and knife parallel on the right side of the plate when you're done. For seating, the host and hostess should be at the opposite ends of the table. Name cards often mark each place setting.

## → Danish Recipes

A popular Danish drink is the Danish Fly. In order to make it, combine one-ounce aquavit, one-ounce banana liqueur, one-ounce fresh lemon juice, and a half-ounce grenadine in a cocktail shaker. Add ice cubes to the shaker, shake well, and fine-strain into a cold pilsner that contains pebbled ice.

 If you want a main course, Kartofler is an exciting option. This meal contains caramelized potatoes. It used to be a meal that was only present in the table of the wealthy. The food was rare because butter and sugar were expensive. However, things are different now.

Leverpostej is a versatile meal that easily stands out as one of the best Danish appetizers. It's usually baked in rectangular pans and can be served chilled or lukewarm. Leverpostej has been known in the art and practice of cooking Danish foods since the mid-19th century. Just like Kartofler, it used to be a meal exclusive to the rich.

Finally, you'll be proud of your decision-making if you choose a homemade green bean casserole as your side dish. During the holiday season, this meal is a superb alternative to cans. Indeed, it requires some effort. However, it'll be worth it to make this delicious and nutritious meal.

# 8 CELEBRATIONS AND SPECIAL MOMENTS

In order to avoid chunking many ideas together in a chapter, this section is a continuation of the previous one. Nevertheless, it offers more details and deeper explanations about the best practices of how to prepare and celebrate special moments.

## HOLIDAY DECORATIONS

Holiday seasons such as Halloween, Thanksgiving Day, Christmas, and Easter offers excellent opportunities to reunite with loved ones. They are the periods of the year when many people who have been on business trips return home to felicitate with their friends and family. There are often get-togethers involving old friends, schoolmates, and other walks of life.

Indeed, living Hygge isn't seasonal but everyday practice. You should not wait until the holidays before you show your loved ones that they mean the world to you. Nonetheless, the holidays offer an ample chance to welcome many people to your home and express your generosity and kindness. The following decoration tips will help you to speak the language of these seasons:

### #Papier-Mache Pinecone Bells

Papier-mache pinecone bells are simple to make but elegant. All you need is some papier mache materials, wires, and small pinecones. The fact that they aren't expensive or stressful but look appealing makes them one of the best choices for a holiday Hygge decoration.

# #Kraft Paper Gift Wrap And Conifer Sprig

This decoration idea is one of the most fantastic ways you can quickly wrap a gift in a typical Hygge format. Get a roll of paper, a sprig of spruce, and traditional painters tape, and you're ready to do some creative things. The best part of using this gift wrap is that you can recycle it, making it the ideal Hygge decoration material.

## #Concrete Hygge Ornaments

Minimalist style ornaments should appeal to you if you want to live the Hygge life. You can paint them all silver, gold, or copper, depending on your taste. Besides, you can choose to leave them blank if you don't want any color. You might also like to stencil snowflakes on these cement rounds for special effects.

# #Dried Orange Star Garland

Orange and clove potpourri ornaments are some of the most elegant things around. They're utterly beautiful and ornate, despite the simplicity and ease it takes to make them. It involves drying the orange peel and making the garland with the aid of a star cookie-cutter.

# #Antique Book Pages Christmas Tree

Getting a giant Christmas tree is excellent because it's in tandem with the spirit of the season. However, it isn't Hygge enough because of the stress involved. Instead of a conventional tree, you can bring some Hygge into your life by choosing an antique book pages' Christmas tree.

It's a fantastic option, especially when you have a small house or a tiny apartment. Moreover, you won't break the bank or sweat making it. Go to a thrift store and pick up like three books. Rip them out and create your tree in no time.

# #Air Dry Clay Dala Horse Ornaments

There's no Nordic Christmas without little wooden Dala horse ornaments. Indeed, they're made of clay, but they have the style of a very traditional wooden figurine that's famous in Scandinavia. Making them is not challenging. Get a cookie-cutter that suits the shape, a black magic marker, and air dry clay to get the job done.

## HOSPITALITY

You cannot separate hospitality from living the Hygge life. Hospitality is the art of hosting and welcoming people to your home. It's often extended to your loved ones. Nonetheless, it's kind of you to also open your home to other people that aren't within your circle of friends and family. When you have celebrations, it's likely that you have uninvited guests.

Sometimes, your invitees might bring their friends and family along. So, it's vital that you learn to deal with both invited and uninvited guests when planning your party. The hacks below will be useful in increasing your hospitality:

→ ## Start From The Scratch

The first thing you need to do before arranging the space is to have an overview of it. Start in the room where you want to host your guests and imagine where the invitees will be sitting. Think about the sizes of the chairs they'll use and how comfortable they'll be.

Imagine your guests eating, drinking, and chatting. Reflect on the lighting fixtures that will be suitable for the occasion. Let the room determine your decoration. The designs should be in harmony with its structure. Creating a Hygge atmosphere isn't restrictive. What matters is understanding and meeting the needs of the guests.

→ ## Moderate Lighting

Your choice of light goes a long way in creating the right ambiance for your visitors. It shouldn't be too dim such that your guests struggle to navigate around. Nonetheless, it shouldn't be too bright such that it lacks the coziness of a Hygge atmosphere. It has to be ideal for the occasion.

Mirrored sconce lighting is a perfect fit for expressing hospitality in the Hygge way. It provides an ambient, soft glow that's in consonance with a Hygge atmosphere. Moreover, this lighting is flattering because it often makes people feel that they look good, thereby enhancing their relaxation and mood.

## → Place A Premium On Comfort

Once your guests aren't comfortable, the hospitality that comes with Hygge living is gone. So, you must place a premium on the comfort of those coming around. Note that seating arrangements play a significant role in how cozy the space feels. You should avoid overcrowding.

It doesn't matter whether those coming around will be sitting on benches, chairs, or stools. Ensure that they aren't stressed. You can leverage a soft velvet fabric to give the chairs a touch of comfort and luxury. Therefore, the guests will be able to plant themselves in the seats for a while.

## → Plan For Unexpected Guests

If your party or celebration is not strictly by invitation, you must plan for unexpected guests. So, you'll have to involve them in all steps of party preparation. In other words, think about them when deciding the number of seats that will be available.

You'll also plan for them when cooking. A little excess for such people won't be a bad idea. It's a sign of a large heart when uninvited guests come for your party, and they don't feel left out of the celebration.

Tyrants and oppressors are always afraid of people with a unified front. It's difficult to defeat a group of people when they share common goals and identity. However, when a set of people aren't united, it's easy to destroy them. Hygge life promotes unity because it's a strength and valuable quality to possess in a group.

It's vital that you and your friends live in harmony. This quality is also integral in a family. Nonetheless, it doesn't happen automatically. You have to take deliberate steps to create togetherness among your friends and family. The tips below will help you in this regard:

# #Prepare And Eat Chili With Friends

A big pot of chili and some cornbread will put you and your friends in the right mood, especially during fall. You can choose meaty or vegetarian chili. They both taste good enough to share with friends. This meal is a fantastic choice when inviting your loved ones over to your house.

Enjoy the food as you take note of the crisp autumn air. This meal is not only tasty but also nutritious. You can get creative with it by adding your favorite condiments for a personal touch.

## #Play Copenhagen

This Nordic game is one of the easiest ways to experience the Hygge feeling in the company of friends and family. Two or four players can play it within 20 to 40minutes. It involves designing new façades for the colorful houses on Nyhavn.

The aim is to ensure that the designs fit seamlessly into the beautiful harbor setting. There are cards on display that the players will use to design their houses after receiving the corresponding façade polyomino tiles.

## #Cozy Conversation In Pleasant Company

This is more than a regular conversation. It's a game that has more than 300 exciting questions that are designed to initiate cozy conversations. Therefore, it sets you and your loved ones in the mood for the ultimate Hygge experience. The objective of this game is to bring people together to share stories and discuss both trivial and crucial parts of their lives.

## BEST RECIPES FOR COMPANY

There are various ways you can strengthen your relationship with your friends and family. One of them is by spending time together where you share food. Eating together creates a unique atmosphere of love and affection where everyone feels welcome and accepted. There are many Danish meals you can share with your loved ones. Here are some of them:

## #Culottesteg

This Danish meal is traditionally prepared with lean, boneless beef steak – sirloin cap. Usually, the rind is left on the steak and the whole cut is often marinated or rubbed with various herbs and spices.

## Ingredients:
2 lbs. Wagyu Black Grade Culotte
Olive oil
Kosher salt
Pepper
4 Tbsps. butter
1/2 onion
1 cup beef broth
3/4 cup red wine
1/2 tsp. sugar
Salt Lick Dry Rub
2 Tbsps. flour

## Directions:
Preheat your oven to 425 F degrees Fahrenheit (220 C).

Place your culotte in a roasting pan. Drizzle your culotte with olive oil and then season with salt, pepper, and Salt Lick Dry Rub.

Roast 15 minutes.

Reduce the heat to 350 degrees Fahrenheit (180 C). Continue to roast for 40-60 minutes or until the internal temperature is 145 degrees.

While the meat roasts, make your red wine sauce. In a medium pan, heat 4 Tbsps. of butter and your onions on medium heat until fragrant (1-2 minutes). Add beef broth, wine, sugar, and a pinch of salt and pepper. Bring to a boil, stirring occasionally.

Once boiling, reduce the heat to low, add 2 Tbsps. of flour, cover, and simmer for approximately 30 minutes or until the sauce thickens.

Let the meat rest 3 minutes, and then slice against the grain. Serve with the sauce.

*__Enjoy!__*

# #Millionbøf

You cannot resist the sight of good millionbøf. In English, it means "million steaks." It's a comforting Danish dish consisting ground beef that's stewed alongside onions and other spices.

## *__Ingredients:__*
1 tablespoon butter
400 g ground beef (about 1 pound)
2 onions, chopped
3 bay leaves
400 ml beef stock
salt & pepper to taste
kulør (gravy browning)
For thickening:
100 ml water (mix with the flour, to thicken the sauce)
2 tablespoons all-purpose flour

a pinch of salt

### *Directions:*

Saute the onions in the golden brown butter. When they start taking color, add the ground beef, and brown it well. This is an important process to create flavor. Add beef stock, bay leaves, and pepper. Let it simmer for about 20-30 minutes with the lid on. Stir occasionally. Mix the water and flour and add some of it in the million beef while whisking, add more until you have the desired consistency; not to runny and not too thick. Season it with salt and pepper, and add the gravy browning.

Serve it with mashed potatoes and pickled beets.

### *Enjoy!*

# #Krebinetter

This food is one of the tastiest and nutritious in the world. It is a versatile meal that features in various places and different settings. You'll want to eat more after the first bite. It's a thick meat patty that's often made with minced pork and veal.

## Ingredients:
1 lb. ground pork
2 tsp. chopped parsley
1 tsp. salt
1 egg
3-4 tbsp. bread crumbs
Flour
Salt & pepper
Butter for frying

## Directions:
Mix the meat with the spices, parsley, salt, egg and bread crumbs. Separate the meat into 4 portions. Make each portion into a ball. Flatten each ball with your hand. Use a knife to crisscross the top of each karbonade while holding its shape with the other hand. Turn the karbonader in the spiced flour. Brown the butter in a frying pan and brown the karbonader. Turn down the heat and fry for 6 minutes on each side.

## Enjoy!

# #Braised Short Ribs

Spice up the day with short ribs to have a full Hygge feeling. It's a fantastic option if you need something you can eat as you curl up on the couch to enjoy the Hygge life. Nonetheless, it's a great way to share with your friends while playing games.

## Ingredients:

5 pounds bone-in beef short ribs, cut crosswise into 2-inch pieces

Salt and black pepper

3 tablespoons vegetable oil

3 medium onions, chopped

3 medium carrots, peeled, chopped

2 celery stalks, chopped

3 tablespoons all-purpose flour

1 tablespoon tomato paste

1 750 ml bottle dry red wine (preferably Cabernet Sauvignon)

10 sprigs flat-leaf parsley

8 sprigs thyme

4 sprigs oregano

2 sprigs rosemary

2 fresh or dried bay leaves

1 head of garlic, halved crosswise

4 cups low-salt beef stock

## Directions:

Preheat oven to 350 F (180 C). Season short ribs with salt and pepper. Heat the oil in a large Dutch oven over medium-high. Working in 2 batches, brown short ribs on all sides, about 8 minutes per batch. Transfer short ribs to a plate. Pour off all but 3 Tbsp. drippings from pot.

Add the onions, carrots, and celery to pot and cook over medium-high heat, stirring often, until onions are browned, about 5 minutes. Add flour and tomato paste; cook, stirring constantly, until well combined and deep red, 2-3 minutes. Stir in wine, and then add short ribs with any accumulated juices. Bring to a boil; lower heat to medium and simmer until wine is reduced by half, about 25 minutes. Add all herbs to pot along with garlic. Stir in the stock. Bring to a boil, cover, and transfer to oven.

Cook until the short ribs are tender, 2–2½ hours. Transfer the short ribs to a platter. Strain the sauce from the pot into a measuring cup. Spoon the fat from surface of sauce and discard; season the sauce to taste with salt and pepper. Serve in shallow bowls over mashed potatoes with the sauce spooned over.
*Enjoy!*

# #Stegte Sild

It's a savory fried pickled herring, which is a classic Danish delight. It's characterized by its mild acidity and tender texture, making it tempting to the taste buds.

## Ingredients:

6 herring fillets (approx. 500 grams)
butter for frying
1 dl rye flour
salt
pepper
4 dl vinegar
3 dl sugar
1 - 2 dl water (optional)
10 black peppercorns
1 onion cut into slices

## Directions:

Cut the dorsal fin off the herring fillets, mix the rye flour with salt and pepper, and then turn the herring fillets into the spicy rye flour. Fold them lengthwise and fry them in butter for about four minutes on each side.

While the herring fillets are cooling, give vinegar, sugar, water and peppercorns a short boil so that the sugar melts. Then let it cool down a bit. Place the herring fillets and onion rings layer by layer in a container, pour the layer over, cover, and refrigerate until eaten. To get the best result, the herring fillets may need to soak a few days on the sheet before being eaten.

***Enjoy!***

# #Sugar Buns

You can prepare this meal in less than an hour. Besides, you only need ten ingredients to make it. Therefore, it's an excellent choice if you need a delicious meal that won't be time-consuming. To have the best experience with this sweet, decadent bun, get a mug of coffee or hot cocoa.

## *Ingredients:*
1/2 cup butter
1/2 cup sugar
1/2 cup raisins
1 cup water

1 large egg
1/2 tsp lemon essence
2 cups plain flour
2 tsp baking powder
1/2 tsp salt
1 tbs white sugar to decorate

### Directions:

Preheat oven to 400 F (200C). Grease or line a baking tray.

Melt butter, sugar, sultanas and water in a microwave and leave to cool.

Sift together flour, baking powder and salt.

Whisk egg and lemon essence in a bowl and add to the cooled butter mixture.

Combine wet and dry ingredients and stir until mixed.

Place large spoonfuls on prepared tray and sprinkle with sugar.

Bake for 15 mins.

### Enjoy!

Indeed, as you may have noticed so far, there are many indoor activities that can bring the Hygge experience. You can spend time alone or with your loved ones doing cozy indoor activities. Nonetheless, outdoor activities are the main art of Hygge life.

Even when you're indoors, one of the ways to bring Hygge into your life is by bringing an outdoor touch such as natural elements like flowers into your home. Therefore, it's vital that you understand how you can improve the quality of your life by staying outdoors as much as possible. This chapter will do justice to that.

## CLOSE TO NATURE

One of the symptoms of depression is social withdrawal. Social withdrawal involves staying away from other people and staying more indoors. So, it isn't a good sign when you spend most parts of your day alone on your bed or couch. Staying outdoors offers you many benefits. For example, accessibility to everyday green inspires you to get out of the door more often, which bodes well for your mental health. More so, staying close to nature helps you to reduce stress. You will be more relaxed as you walk around viewing scenes of nature. It takes away the feelings of fear, anger, and other negative emotions. When you don't have these feelings, you'll increase your chances of moderate blood pressure, muscle tension, and heart rate. These benefits ensure that you live a longer and fuller life.

According to a 2015 study[xi] , walking around and viewing nature improves short-term and working memory by 20%. This study compared a set of participants who walked around a natural environment with people who walked along a busy street. The participants who viewed nature were better in terms of their recall of certain events.

Furthermore, staying close to nature reduces inflammation and has a positive impact on hypertension, according to a 2014 study[xii]. The research explored the therapeutic effect of nature on human hypertension in the elderly. The result of the research showed that forest bathing has medicinal qualities. It inhibits inflammation and offers efficacy against cardiovascular disorders.

In order to stay closer to nature and enjoy its benefits, employ the following tactics:

 **Use Every Moment**

You can set apart a particular day or period of the day when you walk around nature. However, you don't have to go through that route. You can take advantage of every moment to enjoy the fresh air and observe the beauty of nature. For example, you can get up early and go outside for morning exercise even on a working day.

It doesn't matter whether you live in a metropolis or the countryside. The only reason or excuse for not doing anything important is choosing not to do it. If it matters to you that you enjoy the serenity and tranquility nature offers you, you can rearrange your schedule to incorporate it into your daily activities.

→ **Walk To Work**

Technological advancement is meant to be a blessing, but it has become a curse for many people. Besides, many people are in meaningless and futile competition with other people. For example, many people want to ride a car to earn the respect of their neighbors. Indeed, there is nothing wrong with possessing a good ride. However, it should be for the purpose of going to places that are too distant for you. If your workplace isn't far from your home, there is no point in driving your car there just to create an impression. Of course, you can take it along if you feel you might need to go for an official assignment while at work. However, you can just walk to work in the morning to have more vitamin D in your body system. According to a 2014 study[xiii], vitamin D3 improves your mood, thereby making you happier.

## → Use Every Break At Work To Go Outside

Staying with your colleagues during your break at work to share food or discuss interesting topics is excellent. Nonetheless, you can also spend your off time on outdoor activities. For example, you can just take a walk. It gets better when a colleague is willing to walk along with you.

This activity is vital, especially if your office is far from your home, thereby not allowing you to walk there. Your breaks are the best periods for you to stay close to nature and just breathe in the fresh air. Observe every curve and length and just appreciate the creativity in nature. This approach will improve your mood, and consequently, your productivity and job satisfaction.

## → Toasting Marshmallows On A Campfire

Life isn't all about longevity but in moments. I'd rather live a life full of memorable and remarkable ones rather than a long one full of sad moments and negative feelings. Indeed, there's not much you can do about the circumstances that come your way. However, you can decide your response to them and the kind of things you want to do with your life.

One of the ways you can create memorable moments with your loved ones is by toasting marshmallows on a campfire. It provides you the chance to share something in common while having something delectable for your palette at the same time.

## → A Fun Day At The Beach

Water is invigorating. It's full of life with many things buzzing and exciting you. The sight of the rhythmic wave pattern of the sea movement is enough to occupy you. Even if you aren't interested in doing anything but just watch people ride the waves, you'll have enough entertainment and relaxation.

The seaside allows you to engage all your senses and appreciate them. You'll have beautiful sights for your eyes and brilliant sensations due to the relaxing breeze that offers you a calm atmosphere. If you've never been to the sea before, try it one of these days. You might want to do more of that after one trial. If you don't have a sea close by, you can go to a lake or river.

## OUTDOOR ACTIVITIES

If you choose to create a special time in the day or during the weekend to engage in outdoor activities, there are a plethora of options. Below are some fantastic ideas for outdoor activities during the weekend and working days:

## #Outdoor Picnic

If you've never experienced the feeling of having dinner with your loved ones outside, you're missing a lot. Of course, this is best for summer. You can invite your friends over or just have a meal with your family.

Set a dining table at your backyard and lay your favorite blanket.

Get some bottles of fine chilled wine and enjoy the cool of the evening outside with your loved ones. If you can get a variety of wooden boards and bowls to display the food, it makes the experience better. Wooden boards and bowls are better for creating a Hygge atmosphere than plastic cups and plates.

# #Enjoy Time In Nature

I've already mentioned some of the advantages of spending time in nature. If you live in the mountains, hikes and bikes are some of the best activities you can enjoy during the weekend. On the evening of a working day, you can engage in soccer or any sports with your friends. Those let loose moments help you appreciate the simplicity of life, and they improve your mental health.

Nature makes you feel content and calm. Therefore, you'll be doing yourself a lot of good by immersing outdoors. Have more time when you leave your phone at home and spend time outdoors with your friends and family. You can just call a friend you have not seen for a while and take a stroll in a garden as you make up for lost times.

# #Pick Apples Together

One of the fun ways you can spend a fall Hygge day with your friends and family is by going to pick apples together. Plan the day with them. Then go home and have a cooking party to make the most of your collection. This moment also offers you and your loved ones the perfect opportunity to click some photographs.

You can enjoy your spoils of the day by making apple piers, applesauce, cider, and baked apples. If you're lucky enough to have apple trees close to your homes, things will be easier for you and your loved ones.

# #Plant

Planting tulips or any other plant as a family project is Hygge is many ways. It brings the family together to work as a team to try to achieve something. You'll all contribute to the success one way or the other, which makes every family member feel important.

You'll all savor the moments as you watch them grow. The magical display of blooms is an exciting sight and topic you can engage in during your leisure periods. The collective effort improves the mood of every member of the family. Besides, it reminds you of the importance of harmony and teamwork, which are vital components of Hygge life.

# ALL YEAR ROUND – HYGGE FOR ALL SEASONS

According to Meik Wiking, the author of The Little Book of Hygge, Hygge is an everyday pursuit of happiness. You can't force yourself to experience the Hygge feeling. You just have to relax, sit back, and let the emotions overwhelm you. Nonetheless, you can do things that improve your chances of experiencing this feeling of contentment and happiness.

You cannot assign Hygge to any season. In Denmark, it is often cold. So, the Danes usually have a lot of indoor activities to reach inward for happiness. Nonetheless, there's always a plan to experience Hygge for all seasons. You have to plan for both winter and summer. Design Hygge activities for each of these seasons. This technique is the best way of ensuring that you are usually in a good mood all year long.

Have a clear idea of what you need to do during the summer while still in winter. In the same way, you should have activities slated out for summer while still in winter. Below are sample activities that suit different seasons that can bring more Hygge into your life:

## Spring

This part of the year after winter, in which vegetation begins to appear before summer. is perfect for different Hygge activities. Picnics are during this season. You won't find it challenging to find the ideal meal and drink you can share with your family and friends while enjoying the fresh air outdoors.

If you love boating, spring is the best time to explore the waters. This activity is one of the best ways you can unwind during the weekend and ease off the stress of the week. It'll also help you to be in the right physical and mental state as you prepare for the hassle of the new week. You can also consider bicycle rides and outdoor games like tennis and badminton.

## Summer

Summer is refreshing for many reasons. It's the period of the year when the weather is the warmest. Many outdoor events, parties, and camping are usually slated for this time of year. There won't be a fear of rainfall disrupting things. So, it's the best part of the year for many Hygge activities outdoor.

Swimming is the favorite option for many people. Unlike in winter, the weather is warm. Therefore, swimming is one of the best ways to enjoy a cool temperature. Another refreshing and exciting thing you can do during the summer is kayaking. It makes you closer to nature as you enjoy the ride under the sunshine.

Volleyball is another outdoor activity you can try in the summer that brings so much positive vibe. Besides, outdoor yoga and Frisbee are other fantastic options you can consider to have memorable times with your loved ones during the summer.

## Winter

According to Alfred Wainwright, there's no such a thing as bad weather, only unsuitable clothing. Winter is the coldest part of the year. However, it isn't bad weather. In fact, it's the best period for some exciting

Hygge activities that wouldn't have been possible or worthwhile during other seasons.

For example, it's the ideal season for sledding and skiing. Travel over the snow and enjoy the ride downhill to create moments you will remember for a long time. Winter is also the perfect season for skating and making a snowman.

## Autumn

The season after summer before winter is also an ideal time for some outdoor Hygge activities. For example, it's excellent for collecting lives while walking in the bouquet. So, there's no part of the year that doesn't allow you to experience the Hygge feeling. It's all about making plans and executing them.

If you want your friends and family to join you, ensure that you inform them ahead of time so that they can plan for it. Every activity becomes more enjoyable when you have it with your loved ones.

# PART 3 – TOOLS

## 10 START YOUR HYGGENESS LIFE NOW

The best time to start whatever you need to do is now! According to the theory of most common successful books, if you decide to change something, take the first three to five steps immediately to take action towards the goal. Often, people are too lazy to start doing something or are stuck in analyzing the information, and the process becomes longer and longer. I'll encourage you to start your Hygge living with the words of Richard Branson, "Screw it. Let's do it."

### WHY IT'S IMPORTANT TO START IMMEDIATELY

The reason people delay practices such as meditation, exercises, and Hygge living is that they don't see it the same way as medications. Besides, many fail to see what can go wrong when they don't start the practice immediately. If your doctor gives you a drug that can cure your migraine, it's not likely that you delay it until the following month. Why? You know that the problem won't be solved unless you take the medication. You'll keep suffering from the problem until you take the drug.

Besides, the situation can get worse if you don't do something as soon as possible. In the same way, when you are not living the Hygge life, there are negative situations in your life you will keep managing. If care isn't taken, things will get worse until there's no remedy again. Below are some of the advantages of living the Hygge life immediately:

## A New Lease Of Life

The Hygge life gives you a new lease of life, thanks to the transformation it brings to your home and to your life. You will reduce the clutters in your home and opt for a simpler but functional system. Therefore, you'll have more breathing space in a new look home that makes you happy.

Further delays ensure that you'll never enjoy this benefit. You'll keep scrambling for space in your home with disorganized and displaced items. Besides, you might keep struggling with your relationship with your loved ones. They may see you as a snob because of your poor relationship with them. Consequently, they'll want to keep their distance from you.

## Yes To Healthy Living

In any poll, most people will say that their health is more important to them than money or other things. Nonetheless, the approach of many people doesn't demonstrate that. Many people work jobs that don't respect and value their wellbeing. This situation isn't ideal, but this is the reality of the life of many people. Note that health isn't just the absence of a physical ailment, according to the World Health Organization definition. According to this reputable association, health is not complete when you have deficiencies in your state of mind and social relationship. Therefore, to embrace healthy living, you must place a premium on your physical health, mental health, and relationships with the people in your life.

## FIRST 5 STEPS FOR A QUICK START TO A SUCCESSFUL HYGGE LIFE

Hygge life is simple. Remember that it doesn't involve purchasing expensive items. It's vital that you start immediately so that you can begin leveraging the advantages for a happier and fulfilled life. The steps below will help you in this regard:

## #1 Take A Test Of Your Hyggeness Now

The first thing you need to do after deciding to live the Hygge life is to evaluate the level of Hyggeness in your life. This test will enable you to know where you are and how fast you need to improve. Remember that the level of Hyggeness in your life determines the benefits you'll enjoy.

When taking a medication, you need enough doses of the drug to enjoy its therapeutic effect. In the same way, you need a significant amount of Hygge in your life to benefit from its numerous and famous advantages. So, start by taking the test in order to know what you need to do next.

# #2 Analyze What You'd Like To Change/Solve Now

Regardless of your Hygge score, you need to make improvements. You'll need to act faster and do more if you have a low grade. Take your time to think about the things you need to change to improve the level of Hyggeness in your life. It's possible that you need to bring in more flowers and other natural elements to improve the atmosphere of your home.

You may also need to improve the amount of time you should be spending with your loved ones. After your analysis, you may also realize that you're abusing the use of your digital devices. Regardless of your findings, what matters is to highlight areas you need to make changes, and the problems you need to solve, such as digital addiction.

# #3 Make A To-Do List Of 25 Things

Once you realize the areas you need to make improvements, you need to create a to-do list. This list will help you to give direction to your actions. It'll enable to transform your objectives into an actionable plan. Your to-do list may be heavy on decluttering or staying closer to nature as the case may be.

Note that the list does not have to include tasks you must accomplish in a day. It might be a list of activities for a week or even a month. Nonetheless, you need it to have a clear picture of the things you need to do. You might show it to your loved ones or colleague for the sake of accountability. They'll ask you later if you've done them, and that will spur you to action if your progress is stalling.

## #4 Carry Out the First Point From The List

The ultimate essence of creating the list is so that you can carry them out. There's no point in drawing a plan if you won't implement it. So, you must ensure that your list isn't just scribbling on a paper for the sake of it. You need to carry out the plans to enjoy the benefits of living the Hygge life.

One of the ways you can ensure that you carry out your plan is to make the first thing on the list something you can do immediately. If you execute the first task the next day, you may not have the same drive and motivation you have today. So, ensure that you start immediately by performing the first task on the list. This action will set the tone for subsequent activities.

## #5 Make A Playlist For 10 Best Songs You Like More

Doing what makes you happy is crucial to Hygge living. Therefore, you should ensure that you have activities you do daily that reduces your stress and put you in a good mood. Creating a playlist of songs you like is one of the ways you can brighten your mood. If you don't have the songs, download them. Then create the playlist on your phone for them.

It is advisable that you have songs that remind you about the simplicity of life and the value of treating people right. Don't just choose a song that has a good melody. Endeavor to combine an upbeat melody with inspiring lyrics.

## #6 Dance, Cook, Or Paint

Don't just create the playlist; you should find something fun to do. Do something that won't require you to use your intellect a lot. Spend time cooking, dancing, or painting, depending on what you like. Enjoy your playlist while doing this activity. Let the splendid tunes fill the air while you let loose doing what you enjoy.

It's evident that it's easy to start the Hygge life. It's also not challenging to be consistent because it doesn't involve strenuous activities. So, you have no excuse not to start now!

It's one thing to understand the benefits of living the Hygge life; it's another thing to make a deliberate attempt to live it. The aim of this chapter is to give you the right tools that will motivate you to action.

## CHECKLIST OF CHANGES FOR HYGGE/COZY HOME

You can transform your home into that cozy abode that makes you proud by ticking off the following on your list:

### 1. Add Candles To The Interiors

You can change the look of the atmosphere of your home by adding some candlelight to clean, fresh interiors. This design will give your home the cozy, flickering escapes you desire. Moreover, this is one of the easiest ways to create a Hygge ambiance in your home.

Change the atmosphere of your home by letting sweet fragrance fill the air. An easy way to achieve this objective is by bringing in scented candles into your home. It makes your home feel cozy. You just want to stay there and enjoy the moment.

### 2. Change And Add Texture

The texture of the components of your home is a vital ingredient for determining its atmosphere. Consider chunky knit or faux fur throws and cushions. Also, choose fluffy woolen rugs. They're fantastic for creating a cozy, warm interior that will make you, your family, and your guests feel comfortable in your home.

## 3. Put Up Family Photos

Family photos remind you of one of the most important things in life – family. Looking at the pictures on the wall can remind you to be patient and forgiving when members of your family offend you. You'll want to let go to ensure that nothing tears the family apart. Remember that one of the aims of living the Hygge life is to achieve harmony and unity between friends and family.

## 4. Spring Clean And Declutter

I've earlier mentioned the benefits of decluttering your home. This is one of the best ways you can make your life simpler to experience the Hygge feeling. You'll feel proud of yourself when you realize that you don't have anything you don't need in your home. Note that the desire to keep what you don't need can eventually lead to a psychological disorder related to hoarding.

## 5. Store Winter And Heavy Blankets Away

One of the ways you can have more breathing space in your home is by storing away what you don't need at the moment. It isn't every time that you need to give away items to declutter your home. Sometimes, the crowded nature of your home may be because you have items you don't need immediately flying around your home.

For example, you should store away winter blankets during the summer. Bring them back again when you need them to give you the cozy feeling you crave in the next winter.

## 6. Bring Flowers And Plants Indoors

Natural elements like plants and flowers give your home a unique look while reminding you of the importance of staying close to nature. They aren't expensive. However, they can give you something money can never buy – the Hygge experience.

## 7. Open The Windows

You might never realize the difference it makes until you open your windows more. Windows are needed for cross ventilation. Therefore, you defeat their essence when you're fond of closing them. Add this activity to your checklist and let fresh air come into your home. It can tremendously reduce your stress and improve your health.

### CHECKLIST FOR PREPARING FOR HOSTING GUESTS

You need to learn to be an excellent host to live the Hygge life. Opening your doors to your friends and family is an essential part of Hygge living. Your checklist should contain the following:

⇒ **#1 Wash All Guest Bedding**

You don't want your guests to have a wrong impression of you, especially if they won't be leaving on the day they arrive. So, ensure that you wash all guests' bedding before they arrive. Besides, you should neatly make guests' beds.

⇒ **#2 Thoroughly Vacuum And Clean Guest Areas**

Your home should be as comfortable as possible for your guests. Have you been to a place where you were hosted in dirty surroundings? Did you feel comfortable? I'm sure you did not! Therefore, you should give your invitees a comfortable and cozy environment by cleaning the place before their arrival.

⇒ **#3 Scrub Guest Bathrooms**

Of course, you shouldn't leave their bathroom and toilet out of your cleaning. Wash the toilet inside out. Don't forget the sink, faucet, mirror, and tub too. Get the place sparkling clean to make them glad they came around. Never make the wrong impression. The negative remarks that can come from that aren't good for your mental health.

⇒ **#4 Clean All Common Areas**

Don't spend all your energy on the party space, bathroom, and toilet. Also, ensure that you clean other places like your kitchen and living room. Don't give your guests the impression that you're only pretending to be clean because they're around. You should give your house a better look before they arrive.

## ⇒        #5 Create Space For Luggage

It's imperative that your visitors have somewhere to keep their luggage. You should also ensure that they have somewhere they can store their clothes. Your home shouldn't become messy and inhabitable because your friends and family visited.

## ⇒        #6 Stock Up The Bathroom

Don't only plan for their food. You should also prepare for other necessities. For example, you should stock up their bathroom with soap, toothpaste, and toilet paper. Make your house a home away from home for them during their stay.

## ⇒        #7 Pick Up Some Extras

You can also buy some extra items just in case your guests need them. To illustrate, you can purchase toothbrushes, razors, antacids, and aspirin tablets. Your visitors may need them, and they'll be grateful if you can provide them.

## ⇒        #8 Snacks, Foods, And Drinks

These are essential to hosting people. Therefore, it must never go missing on your checklist. It isn't an ideal situation when your guests have to use their money to purchase food while staying at your place. So, apart from ensuring that they stay in a friendly and comfortable environment, you need to cater to their meals too.

# CHECKLIST OF SERVING DINNER

If you're hosting your friends and family for dinner, you need to address the following things:

⇒     **#1 Buy Perishables**

You need to purchase perishables a day before the event to avoid having to rush to get them.

⇒     **#2 Defrost Frozen Food**

It's vital that the frozen foods are ready a day ahead of the dinner. This approach will help you avoid the stress of making them available the next day.

⇒     **#3 Prepare Sauces, fillings, and Soups**

Of course, you need to cook whatever will be eaten before the arrival of the guests. You should be thinking more about serving them and putting on a good outfit rather than cooking by the time they arrive.

⇒     **#4 Pick Up Flowers**

Your visitors can learn to live the Hygge life from you. Add beautiful flowers to your decorations to add natural beauty to the event.

⇒     **#5 Make Ready Chilled Drinks**

Apart from food, your guests need drinks also. So, you should make chilled ones ready before they come around. Ensure that you know the preferred drinks of your visitors. You can stock both alcoholic and non-alcoholic drinks if you have guests who will want either of the two.

⇒ **#6 Chop, Peel, and Prepare Vegetables And Fruits**

You should add fruits and vegetables to the meal. They offer nutritious value, which bodes well for the health of your guests. So, prepare them ahead of time.

⇒ **#7 Set The Table**

The table should be ready before your visitor comes around. It isn't ideal to start spreading the tablecloth or any other thing you need to do to make the table ready in the presence of the guests.

⇒ **#8 Charge Camera Battery**

Dinners are opportunities to create pleasant memories. So, get your camera ready if you won't need a professional photographer. Some clicks won't hurt.

⇒ **#9 Stock Extra Roll Of Toilet Paper**

Your guests might urgently need to use the toilet before they go home. Ensure you prepare for that.

## MONTHLY CHECKLIST OF CLUTTER-FREE/CLEANING

You can have a monthly plan to declutter and clean your home. In a particular month, your checklist can look like this:

⇒ **Put Away The Decors**

Your home can be a mess, thanks to unused and unnecessary decors. This disorganization often occurs after celebrations such as Christmas, Thanksgiving,

Halloween, or Easter. There's a tendency to leave the decorations long after those festivals. So, at the end of the month of the celebration, you can plan to remove them and either store them away or throw them away.

⇒ **Store The Books**

It's good to have a reading culture. However, you can make your home uncomfortable when you have books in places they should not be found. So, the end of the month is ideal for bringing back some sanity to your home.

⇒ **Give Away Duplicate Items**

It's possible that someone presents an item you already possess to you as a gift. You may never need to use them, and they will end up forming clutters in your home. To avoid such a situation, give away such items. Such a kind gesture is a quick way to experience the Hygge feeling.

⇒ **Throw Off Broken Items**

In some cases, you may be able to repair some items. If that is the case, do so. However, you don't need to remind yourself of your loss by keeping broken items in your home. Make plans to throw them away when decluttering your home at the end of the month.

⇒ **Discard Expired Paints And Chemicals**

Just like broken items, you should dispose of expired paints and chemicals. There's no point in keeping them in your home when they're useless.

⇒ **Purge Drawers**

Your drawers can be full of unneeded items if you don't check them. The end of the month is perfect for checking through them to ensure that you only have the things that you need in them.

## HYGGE ACTIVITIES FOR DIFFERENT SEASONS

I've formerly given you Hygge ideas for different seasons. Nonetheless, there are some Hygge activities that you need, regardless of the period of the year.

⇒ **Disconnect!**

There are many books and articles about digital detoxification because of its benefits. You need to learn to let go of your devices and get more out of life. If you often feel like something is wrong with you whenever you aren't with your phone, you need to disconnect as soon as possible. You can avoid visiting your social media page for a week for a start.

⇒ **Prioritize Comfort When Dressing**

Being comfortable is crucial to the Hygge life. Therefore, you should not compromise on your comfort, even when dressing. Many luxurious and expensive outfits out there makes you look good but make you feel uncomfortable. Reduce your stress level by always wearing outfits that give you an appealing appearance without making you feel bad.

⇒ **Value Yourself**

When you have low self-esteem, you cannot experience the Hygge feeling. You should see yourself as a valuable person that deserves the love and respect of other people. Others may not appreciate you, but you must always consider yourself as a unique individual who deserves to be treated well. So, spoil yourself once in a while with nice meals and soothing baths.

⇒    **Get Baking**

Learn to make homemade cakes, bread, and cookies. The Danes are renowned for their knack of baking and eating homemade pastries and bread. The satisfaction of making something delicious can be a free therapy that can restore your self-confidence and reduce your anxiety levels.

# 10 DAYS FULL OF HYGGE

This is the last part of this wonderful journey. So, it's logical that we end it by giving you a straightforward plan as you start. The main idea of this chapter is to call you to action by providing information that can help you declutter your home and create the Hygge atmosphere. Below is a typical 10 days plan that will transform your home, and consequently, your life.

## DAY 1: START FROM EASY THINGS

Taking things easy is always the best approach to starting anything. Remember that Hygge isn't about what you do but the way you do whatever you're doing. So, you don't need to do something spectacular, especially on the first day. On the first day of practicing Hygge, you can plan to wake up 30 minutes earlier than usual, especially on a workday. Your alarm will come in handy in this regard to avoid oversleeping.

When you're awake, have a morning exercise. You can just stretch. For more simple exercises, you can check the internet. You'll easily find a plethora of options. If your workplace isn't far from home, you can walk to work and enjoy nature. You'll also get some vitamin D alongside. Besides, it might be an opportunity to see your city in a new light as you watch people try to go to work in the morning.

## DAY 2: SET A TABLE IN A BEAUTIFUL, UNUSUAL WAY

Trying a different approach to setting your table can help you experience the Hygge feeling. This activity can help you appreciate your creativity. It'll make you feel good about yourself, especially when you get positive remarks from your friends and families when they see it.

Your loved ones will be taken aback by the new setting when they come around to dine with you.

In order to get the best out of this activity, avoid multitasking. Ensure that you do other things you need to do before or after you're done. Remember that multitasking is one of those factors that can hinder you from experiencing the Hygge feeling. So, apart from this activity, you should avoid doing two or three things simultaneously. Give every activity all of your energy to make the best of it.

## DAY 3: COOK SOME DISH BY A NEW RECIPE

Cooking can be stressful when you are under pressure to fix a meal immediately. However, when you're making a meal for yourself or your loved ones without stress, it is one of the most enjoyable activities you can perform. Besides, you can share the task with other people if you're cooking something that may require an extra hand. Sharing your task with others is a fantastic way of building trust and harmony.

You can make cooking fun by choosing to cook a new meal with a new recipe. It's a learning and experimental process that often ends in a positive mood, regardless of the outcome. You'll be proud of your cooking skills if you manage to pull it off. Nonetheless, you'll have a good laugh with your loved ones if the experiment doesn't end up the way you desire.

## DAY 4: ENJOY A SPA DAY AT HOME

Remember that Hygge trains you to place a premium on your health. Besides, you should also have periods when you unwind by doing your favorite activity. It can involve enjoying a spa at home. You don't need to go somewhere you'll need to pay for it. Set it up at home and make it a ritual you have to cool off at least once in a week.

On that day, endeavor to change the sheets. An aroma bath is also an option worth considering. Employ a scented candle and play some good music to give you a pleasurable day you'll want to have all over again. You can also spend some time reading a book or your favorite magazine. Ensure that you're engrossed in every activity to experience the Hygge feeling while doing them.

## DAY 5: CHECK THE TO-DO LIST

I've reiterated that living the Hygge life improves your productivity. Besides, it improves your time management skills. On the fifth day, revisit your to-do list and look for things you should have done that you have always postponed. For example, you can check your to-do list for cleaning the house. You might have stopped somewhere because of one thing or the other. Carry out the leftover tasks on your free day.

You can experience the Hygge feeling from doing your leftover tasks because it gives you a sense of fulfillment. It makes you feel that you're using your spare time for something productive, and that helps you to generate positive vibes. Meanwhile, you need positive emotions to experience the Hygge feeling. Moreover, it helps your state of mind.

## DAY 6: CLUTTER-FREE DAY

Decluttering your home is an activity that has multiple benefits. It makes your home look neater and also gives you enough space to walk freely in your home. People who have clutters are often like prisoners in their homes. They keep seeing unpleasant sights but wouldn't do anything about them. You shouldn't be like that. You don't have to wait until your home is inhabitable before you do something about it.

Pick a day in the week when you go through your stuff and eliminate unnecessary things taking up space. If they're totally useless, throw them away. However, if they're still useful but you don't need them, give them away. Sharing with other people is one of the ways you can experience the Hygge feeling. So, don't have a culture of hoarding items just for the sake of possessing them.

## DAY 7: REORGANIZE FURNITURE IN ONE SPACE IN YOUR HOME

After some periods of use, your furniture might be here and there in your home. If you don't take time to reorganize them, they can be a source of stress to you. So, take a day to put them back to where they belong. If doing it in every room won't be too stressful, you can start from one room in a day and do another one on another day.

For example, you can start with your living room. Then move to your bedroom some other day. When your furniture isn't in the right order, it'll make your home look disorganized, and that affects its atmosphere. You'll feel that something isn't right. Besides, your visitors will also deem that you aren't a neat person when they come around.

Improve the atmosphere of your home by adding cozy things. To avoid repetition, check chapter seven for some of the things I highlighted that could improve the ambiance of your home. The good news is that none of those things are expensive. That's the beauty of living the Hygge life. You can enrich your mood and your health without spending anything significant.

The fact that you don't need to spend much to be happy shows that living the Hygge life is nature's design for us. Therefore, living Hygge is for everyone. You can make your life more meaningful and beautiful by adding more cozy things to your life. Offer value to yourself and make other people feel appreciated when they come to your home.

## DAY 9: INVITE GUESTS

I've mentioned the benefits of inviting guests before now. It's an integral part of living the Hygge life. Hygge living enables you to open your heart more to other people. Meanwhile, you cannot open your heart without opening your wallet and opening your home. In other words, you can't claim to love people without sharing with them. Hospitality and affection are common attributes of people who live the Hygge life. Remember the preparation checklist and rules. Inviting guests to your home requires you to sacrifice your time, energy, and resources for them. Therefore, you must be mentally prepared for the occasion before you go ahead with the decision. Some people may not appreciate your sacrifice for them. Nonetheless, you shouldn't stop being hospitable for your own sake.

## DAY 10: CHECK YOUR FEELINGS

I'm usually surprised when I ask people what matters to them the most, and they cannot offer definite answers. It might sound ridiculous, but some people have never taken their time to realize what they value the most. Many people aren't sure what motivates them and inspires them the most. If you don't know these things, you'll struggle to experience the Hygge feeling.
Nonetheless, it isn't too late to find out about your feelings. Take time to make a new list of things that inspires you the most. Think about the activities you

like to do that makes you feel alive. Engage in them more. In the same way, think about situations that often stress you out and plan to avoid them.

# CONCLUSION

I'm certain that you have a sound understanding of Hygge by now if you were a novice before now. Even if you knew some things before picking up this book, I'm confident that your understanding of this way of life is now deeper. The Hygge life has been earning rave reviews across Europe for all the right reasons. We all want to live happier and more fulfilled lives, and Hygge offers you the simplicity and decisions needed to achieve your objective. We began by explaining what Hygge is all about. I explained that it's more than an idea or concept but a way of life among the Scandinavians.

We ventured into the history of Hygge, and we saw that this culture is rooted in Danish and Norwegian culture. Nonetheless, the Danes have taken it as their national identity. It's the framework of every sector of their economy and life. We also explained that there's no direct replacement for Hygge in the English vocabulary. Nonetheless, it's associated with coziness, simplicity, fulfillment, harmony, and unity. It's a way of life that has nothing to do with how much you have in your bank account. Hygge is the foundation for the worldview of the Danes, where they believe everyone is equal.

In the subsequent chapter, we looked at the benefits you stand to enjoy by living the Hygge life. We also discussed the Hygge atmosphere. I mentioned that this atmosphere offers inclusiveness, coziness, and homogeneity. Regarding the advantages, we stated that it reduces anxiety by helping you to cope favorably with pressure and expectations. Besides, it helps you to live in the moment and improve your sleep. The Hygge life enhances trust and intimacy between friends and family. It also improves your mood and focus. Moreover, it increases your productivity by enhancing your time management skills.

If you had doubts before now that Hygge may not be for you, that doubt should be gone by now. This life is for everyone because Hygge is in your soul already. I mean, the desire to live a quiet, simple life in the loving arms of our loved ones has been ingrained in us by nature. We become depressed and feel empty when we try to live otherwise. So, you cannot run away from this way of life. Rather, you should only try to understand it better and cultivate this positive culture. People who live the Hygge life pay more attention to their health and the things that matter in life.

We were also able to distinguish between cozy and Hygge. I had to include that chapter because I discovered that many people assume that these concepts are the same. Meanwhile, they're actually worlds apart. Indeed, they both have similarities, such as requiring intentionality and aiming at improving the quality of your life. Nevertheless, they aren't the same. Some of the key differences is that cozy is more individualistic and simple to explain than Hygge. Nonetheless, you don't have to choose between the two. Instead, you can combine them together to have a fulfilled and meaningful life.

In the subsequent chapter, we explored how you can evaluate the level of Hyggeness in your life. With the aid of the smart test, you should know the level of Hyggeness in your life now and how you can improve on it. You can always start from somewhere and get better over time. Choosing the Hygge life means embracing happiness, simplicity, getting your priorities right, and living life on your own terms. Being able to slow down is an integral part of living Hygge, and it is a culture you have to cultivate. I've delivered morning and daily Hygge rituals. Practice them to enhance your experience in life.

I pointed out that Hygge isn't just for your home. It is a tradition you can also have in your workplace. A vital way to do that is by communicating the Hygge way by using more of "we" rather than "I." You need to let your employees feel like valuable members of a team rather than subordinates. I also provided you with tips to create the Hygge atmosphere in our office. It all begins by revamping the environment by making alterations such as the lighting. You should also avoid multitasking and sharing meals with your colleagues during your break as much as possible.

Additionally, we looked at how you can bring Hygge to your home. It all begins by decluttering, which is a beneficial activity that doesn't cost anything. I offered different hints that can make the process easier for you. Ensure you take advantage of them to make your life fuller and more enjoyable. Do you remember Lagom? Having just enough should be your watchword when organizing your home. You shouldn't have furniture or decorations just for the sake of it. You should only have items that are useful to you in your home.

Again, I explained that Hygge is an everyday affair. Nonetheless, you can take advantage of the holiday seasons to bring more Hygge into your life. Leverage those periods to use some simple but brilliant designs that are welcoming to your guests. The holiday seasons are also perfect opportunities to express hospitality by welcoming friends and families to your home. Moreover, outdoor activities are crucial to living the Hygge life. So, incorporate outdoor activities that will allow you to be closer to nature into your life. Plan for all seasons to ensure that you live a happy and fulfilled life all year long.

Finally, don't hesitate to start living the Hygge life now. Leverage the tools and tips I provided to get your life on track by living Hygge. One more day of not living Hygge is one more day of frustration and negative emotions. Leverage the 10 days of Hygge to get started and take it up from there. Remember that your life is a summary of all the moments in them. So, embrace simplicity. Stop taking life too seriously. Smile, get cozy, value your relationships, practice gratitude, and live the Hygge life!

# LEAVE THE REVIEW

As an independent author with a small marketing budget, reviews are my livelihood on this platform. If you enjoyed this book, I'd really appreciate it if you left your honest feedback. I love hearing from my readers and I personally read every single review.

# REFERENCES

[i] Wang et al. Use of mental health services for anxiety, mood, and substance disorders in 17 countries in the WHO world mental health surveys. The Lancet. 2007; 370(9590):841-50

[ii] Gullestad, Marianne (1992). "Home Decoration as Popular Culture". The art of social relations: essays on culture, social action and everyday life in modern Norway. Oslo: Scandinavian University Press. p. 235. ISBN 8200216527. [note 12 for chapter III]

[iii] Falk, Hjalmar & Torp, Alf (1903). "Hu". Etymologisk Ordbog over det norskeog det danske Sprog (in Norwegian). Kristiania: Aschehoug. p. 303. Falk, Hjalmar & Torp, Alf (1903). "Hygge". Etymologisk Ordbog over det norskeog det danske Sprog (in Norwegian). Kristiania: Aschehoug. p. 315

[iv] "Top 10 Collins Words of the Year 2016 - New on the blog – Word Lover's blog - Collins Dictionary". www.collinsdictionary.com. Retrieved 2018-10-11.

[v] Altman, A. (2017, June 19). The Year of Hygge, the Danish Obsession with Getting Cozy. Retrieved September 25, 2020, from https://www.newyorker.com/culture/culture-desk/the-year-of-hygge-the-danish-obsession-with-getting-cozy

[vi] Kristian Næsby | Department of Scandinavian Studies | University of Washington. (n.d.). Retrieved September 25, 2020, from https://scandinavian.washington.edu/people/kristian-naesby

[vii] Helliwell, John; Layard, Richard; Sachs, Jeffrey (April 2, 2012). "World Happiness Report" (PDF). Columbia University Earth Institute. Retrieved 2014-06-29.

[viii] Oldest continuously used national flag. Retrieved September 25, 2020, from https://www.guinnessworldrecords.com/world records/oldest-continuously-used-national-flag/?fb_comment_id=750446551706828_984625741622240

[ix] C40: City of Cyclists Reduces Approximately 90,000 Tons of CO2 Emissions per Year and Has Ov... (2011). Retrieved September 25, 2020, from https://www.c40.org/case_studies/city-of-cyclists-reduces-approximately-90000-tons-of-co2-emissions-per-year-and-has-over-50-of-the-citys-population-cycling-to-work-everyday

[x] Booth, M. (2015, February 12). The 1933 Novel That Scandalized Denmark. Retrieved September 25, 2020, from https://www.theparisreview.org/blog/2015/02/11/the-law-of-jante/

[xi] Patrick, R et al. Vitamin D and the omega-3 fatty acids control serotonin synthesis and action, part 2: relevance for ADHD, bipolar, schizophrenia, and impulsive behavior. FASEB J fj.14-268342; published ahead of print February 24,

2015.https://faseb.onlinelibrary.wiley.com/doi/full/10.1096/fj.14-268342

[xii] Moran, LJ et al. Vitamin D is independently associated with depression in overweight women with and without PCOS. Gynecol Endocrinol. 2014 Nov 4:1-4. http://www.ncbi.nlm.nih.gov/pubmed/25366261

[xiii] Spedding S. Vitamin D and depression: a systematic review and meta-analysis comparing studies with and without biological flaws. Nutrients. 2014 Apr 11;6(4):1501-18. doi: 10.3390/nu6041501. PMID: 24732019; PMCID: PMC4011048.

Made in the USA
Monee, IL
30 December 2021

87554547R00083